PRISONERS OF OUR THOUGHTS

"Here is a   he search
for meani   **DATE DUE**   prove-
ment at a   _____   scription
for promo... FEB 28 2011

—Kenneth R. Pelletier, PhD, MD, Clinical Professor of Medicine &
Professor of Public Health, University of Arizona and UCSF Schools
of Medicine, and author of *Best Alternative Medicine: What Works?
What Does Not?*

"*Prisoners of Our Thoughts* is an important book about creating a meaningful
life—a life that matters and makes a difference. Those of us involved in the
individual quest for meaning will find valuable information and inspiration in it.
Meaning—choosing it, living it, sustaining it—is a significant personal, as well
as societal, issue of the twenty-first century."

—Marita J. Wesely, trends expert and Trends Group Manager, Hallmark
Cards, Inc.

"In the permanent white water of our lives everywhere and especially at work,
the meaning of what we do and of who we are is continually in danger of nega-
tion. The creation of meaning cannot be a once-and-for-all, set-it-and-forget-it
affair, but rather needs to become our most basic ongoing achievement. This
book is virtually unique in providing us with both a philosophy and a set of
methods for keeping the meaning of our lives and our work vibrantly alive, relevant, and nourishing."

—Peter B. Vaill, PhD, Antioch University, and author of *Managing as a
Performing Art*

"Dr. Pattakos has created an important book on the self. His humanity shines
throughout this very practical guide of our consciousness."

—Alki David, actor, film and television producer, Chairman, FilmOn.
com PLC and 111 Pictures Ltd., London, England

"In *Prisoners of Our Thoughts*, Dr. Pattakos does a great job proving that success
does not always mean satisfaction, why it is important to have both in your life,
and how to achieve both."

—Isadore Rosenfeld, MD, Rossi Distinguished Professor of Clinical
Medicine, Weill Cornell Medical College, and medical consultant for
Fox News

"Magical. . . . If you read this book patiently and honestly, it may begin to change
your attitude and thought process. Deeply and impressively subversive in more
ways than one, this book invites us directly, in the search for meaning of our
work and life."

—Ping Fu, founder and CEO of Geomagic, Inc.

"The transcendent spirit of Viktor Frankl vindicated human resilience. Alex
Pattakos nimbly brings essential, new life to that spirit. Reading this book is a
choice—a choice to add deeper meaning to your life."

—Jeffrey K. Zeig, PhD, Director, The Milton H. Erickson Foundation

"Not averse to giving 'recipes,' Pattakos makes them transparent and convincing enough, and he amply supports them by personal observations and experiences, by testimonies and quotations, by anecdotes and proven wisdom, adding more than a sprinkle of wit and common sense. And he does it all in an immensely readable style."

    —Dr. Franz J. Vesely, Viktor Frankl Institute, Vienna, Austria

"Logotherapy was tested in Nazi concentration camps, so it speaks uniquely of meaning in extremes of unavoidable suffering. But Frankl also encouraged the discovery of meaning in our everyday workplaces, and Pattakos offers both a why and a how."

    —Haddon Klingberg, Jr., PhD, author of *When Life Calls Out to Us: The Love and Lifework of Viktor and Elly Frankl*

"If you want to bring life to your personal and/or organizational values—read *Prisoners of Our Thoughts*. It is particularly helpful if you are committed to living an authentic (values-driven) life. This is a book you will want all your associates and family members to read again and again."

    —Ann Rhoades, President, People Ink, and former Executive Vice President, People, JetBlue Airways

"At once a manifesto on the importance of navigating our individual paths with eyes wide open and a road map to a purpose driven life, Pattakos' channeling of Viktor Frankl's writings illuminates 'meaning' as the ultimate value in our work. Dr. Pattakos shows us how gradual shifts in our elemental patterns of thought toward obstacles we may encounter—at work, at home, and in our relationships—can change our lives and consequently the world."

    —Jay Shanker, entertainment industry attorney, business advisor, and law school instructor, and coauthor of *Entertainment Law and Business*

"An incisive, lively book that brings the key tenets of Logotherapy to bear on today's stressful workplace in a very meaningful way. Dr. Pattakos drives home that it is through our power of choice and our choice of attitude that we can transform any workplace or life challenge into a meaningful experience."

    —Carol Willett, Chief Learning Officer, U.S. Government Accountability Office

"It is very rare to encounter a book that is simultaneously profound and approachable, one that addresses the essential crux of the human dilemma in a manner that is inviting and even heartfelt. *Prisoners of Our Thoughts* is just such a book. I highly recommend it."

    —Jeffrey Mishlove, PhD, Dean of Transformational Psychology, University of Philosophical Research, and author of *The Roots of Consciousness*

"Alex Pattakos' brilliant book rocks with power and passion. I have already read it three times and have only begun to absorb the wisdom in these pages. Encore!"

    —Laurie Nadel, PhD, Executive Producer/Host, "The Dr. Laurie Show"/ Genesis Communications Network, and author of *The Sixth Sense*

"*Prisoners of Our Thoughts* demonstrates that understanding meaning-making is a key tenant to authentic leadership in any profession. Learning to nurture the ability to extend beyond oneself builds deeper relationships personally and pro-

fessionally. This book is required reading for anyone seeking to create meaning in their lives."
— Joseph G. Raasch, Deputy Chief Operations Officer, Saint Paul Public Schools, Minnesota

"A must-read for all those who want to lead successful lives.... The book has universal appeal and would help people working in any part of the world, and at any type of job. Dr. Pattakos' concepts resonate well with me — a Sikh by religion. I believe that world peace would be greatly helped by having more and more people happy with their lives, as *Prisoners of Our Thoughts* could help them be."
— Karuna Singh, Program Manager, Office of Public Affairs, U.S. Consulate General, Kolkata, India

"Dr. Pattakos gives us the tools we need to look at our life differently...to break away from the thoughts that limit our potential and to start to live the life we want to live. Building on the work of Dr. Viktor Frankl, he has written an easy-to-read and pragmatic book that inspires us to make positive change in our lives."
— Les Hine, President and CEO, Mxi Technologies, Ottawa, Canada

"A reflective, how-to book for finding meaning in the mundane of everyday life. *Prisoner of Our Thoughts* reminds us that the search for true meaning illuminates our lives with true freedom. The book inspires us to appreciate life and guides the reader's growth and progress with a new balanced scorecard for making life meaningful. Read the book and begin the path toward meaning."
— William V. Flores, PhD, President, University of Houston–Downtown

"Dr. Pattakos explains that we are creatures of habit, who unwittingly lock ourselves into our own mental cages. *Prisoners of Our Thoughts* brings meaning to turbulent times, providing hope for those who are searching for the key to a meaningful life."
— Kelly Jad'on, Founder, www.BasilandSpice.com (syndicated author and book reviews on a healthy life)

"Makes the search for meaning and direction in one's professional and personal life easier to navigate. This guide has been adopted by our entire team, resulting in greater collaboration and breakthrough thinking at every level. An added bonus has been the realization that anyone can benefit from a greater sense of meaning in all facets of their business and everyday life by following the principles of *Prisoners of Our Thoughts*."
— Kevin Finnegan, Executive Vice President, Global Sales and Operations, New York & Company

"Living and working in such changing times takes courage. This book helps us connect with ourselves and meaning in order to be happier, develop resilience in life and work, and co-create a better future. In a time when there is so much unpredictability, *Prisoners of Our Thoughts* is a must-read to serve as a prescription for personal and business leadership."
— Lisa Schilling, RN, MPH, Vice President, Healthcare Performance Improvement, Kaiser Permanente

"Those who seek meaning in their work and life will find much of value in this practical application of the wisdom of Dr. Frankl, so deeply experienced and artfully presented."

—Dee Hock, Founder and CEO Emeritus, VISA, and author of *One from Many: VISA and the Rise of the Chaordic Organization*

"*Prisoners of Our Thoughts* is a must-read. Not only is it written in very direct, clear language to assert the case for each of us to follow the meaning in our lives, but it hits an intuitive nerve as Dr. Pattakos explains Viktor Frankl's sources for authentic meaning in one's life. This has been a major influence in creating a more rewarding life for me and countless others."

—Michael E. Skaggs, Executive Director, Nevada Commission on Economic Development

"Masterpiece. Challenging. Insightful. Motivational. Inspirational. Magnificent. *Prisoners of Our Thoughts* branches all of these into one central theme: staying true to you, the real you. This book is a must-read for all educators, parents, and students. It provides such a clear view of the importance of character and how love ties it all together. A must-read."

—Dr. Mark Isley, Principal, Shelby County Alternative School, Alabama

"I was the person described in every chapter in this wonderfully insightful and reflective book. I intend to read it again and again, especially during those times when my life seems to control me in ways that are troubling to my human spirit."

—Karen Bloom, Chicago, Illinois

"Alex Pattakos does a wonderful job of translating Frankl's work into actions for living. He delivers an especially powerful message for individuals striving to grow both professionally and personally. I can think of no other book that better prepares leaders for facing tough challenges. This is a must-read for leaders!"

—Dr. Mitch Owen, College of Agriculture and Life Sciences, North Carolina State University

"Don't let life just happen to you! Let Dr. Pattakos show you how to apply Viktor Frankl's core principles to make your work—and life—more meaningful. Anyone from mail deliverer to CEO can embark on a path of self-discovery that will lead to better results and relationships with others."

—Jean E. Spence, Executive Vice President, Global Technology and Quality, Kraft Foods

"*Prisoners of Our Thoughts* is an enormously inspiring eye and heart opener, enlarging the scope of our life and work in a wonderful way. It's a book full of wisdom, a road sign to the meaning and riches of life."

—Dr. Heinrich Anker, cofounder, Management Centre Zug (Switzerland), and President, Swiss Society of Logotherapy and Existential Analysis

"Although I am not connected to a workplace setting, reading *Prisoners of Our Thoughts* in a home-based environment had a significant impact and personal meaning to me. The constant need for self-motivation renewal and the courage to

walk your own path came into sharp focus as I contemplated Alex Pattakos' vivid imagery,…a powerful reminder to me to not be satisfied with the status quo and to proactively strive for personal excellence, whatever your circumstance."
— Angela Buschmann, Sydney, Australia

"In *Prisoners of Our Thoughts*, Alex Pattakos draws upon the entire body of Viktor Frankl's work and outlines seven core principles which can be applied to work situations or everyday life. Use *Prisoners of Our Thoughts* as a textbook, order it for all your employees, or buy a copy for yourself."
— Erik Bergrud, Vice President, American Society
for Public Administration

"In bringing Viktor Frankl into the workplace, Pattakos has produced a thoughtful and powerful guide that offers insight and wisdom."
— Alan M. Webber, founding editor, *Fast Company*

"It has been a long wait—a very long wait! But Frankl's principles and methods have at last been set free to be used and enjoyed and practiced in the work situation."
— Dr. Patti Havenga Coetzer, founder, Viktor Frankl Foundation
of South Africa

"A practical and profound must-read for anyone interested in serious self-actualization. Pattakos has brilliantly assimilated and clearly, simply, and usefully explained Frankl's concepts for life fulfillment in seven straightforward, easy-to-use, life-changing principles. In *Prisoners of Our Thoughts*, Pattakos holds the light for anyone wanting to see."
— Richard M. Contino, Esq., author of *Trust Your Gut!*

"If you want to take on life and work with new, refreshed meaning, this is the book to free you from your perceived limitations and open the way for living life and experiencing work in a different way."
— Debbe Kennedy, founder, Global Dialogue Center, and author of
Putting Our Differences to Work

"I fully recommend reading this great work and applying its wisdom. Please don't wait to open your 'lockbox' of talents and tasks that life has set aside for you. Seek what is yours on behalf of all mankind."
— Robert R. Thompson, Lieutenant Colonel, U.S. Army

"Dr. Pattakos provides a common sense model to resolve the existential anxiety created by the gap between our thoughts and reality and to tremendously enrich our lives. Read *Prisoners of Our Thoughts* and be prepared to look in the mirror and see the person responsible for your dissatisfaction and unhappiness!"
— Vann E. Schaffner, MD, Spokane, Washington

"Pattakos has taken Frankl's positive outlook of mankind's potential and, in appealing to the inner 'wisdom of the heart,' encourages business management philosophy to look long and hard at the benefits of these teachings."
— Gregory B. Clark, diplomate, Viktor Frankl Institute of Logotherapy,
and Fellow, American Academy of Experts in Traumatic Stress

"Every thinking person can benefit from the work of Alex Pattakos. As we wind our way through life's challenges, understanding life's choices and outcomes is foremost. This work adds a great deal of value to this most important of life's searches."

—Robert Agranoff, PhD, Professor Emeritus, School of Public and Environmental Affairs, Indiana University Bloomington

"If, like most of us, you hunger for a greater sense of meaning, purpose, and freedom in your life, *Prisoners of Our Thoughts* will provide you with the stories, concepts, and opportunities that will help you break free from old patterns of thought and action."

—Judi Neal, PhD, Director, John H. Tyson Center for Faith and Spirituality in the Workplace, University of Arkansas

"CEOs, as well as the average worker, can be both informed and inspired by Pattakos' book."

—Paul T. P. Wong, PhD, President, International Network on Personal Meaning, Tyndale University College, Toronto, Canada, and coeditor of *The Human Quest for Meaning: A Handbook of Psychological Research and Clinical Applications*

"Today's workplace and home environment are less personal than ever due to the use of information technology, making the need for meaning in everyday life more relevant and more important than ever before. Alex Pattakos has done a masterful job of presenting Viktor Frankl's philosophy and applying it in today's world. An essential read regardless of age, career, or station in life."

—Chris Krahling, President and CEO, New Mexico Mutual

"Do yourself a favor and read *Prisoners of Our Thoughts*. Then share it with and teach it to your employees. I use the teachings of this book in my daily life, and it has made me more productive in good times and has allowed me to break through the negativity in more challenging times."

—Mark Bernhard, PhD, Director, Continuing and Professional Education, Virginia Polytechnic Institute and State University

Viktor Frankl's Principles
for Discovering Meaning in Life and Work

PRISONERS OF OUR THOUGHTS

SECOND EDITION, REVISED AND UPDATED

ALEX PATTAKOS, PhD

BK

Berrett–Koehler Publishers, Inc.
San Francisco
a BK Life book

Berrett-Koehler Publishers, Inc.
235 Montgomery Street, Suite 650
San Francisco, CA 94104-2916
Tel: (415) 288-0260   Fax: (415) 362-2512 www.bkconnection.com

Ordering Information

Quantity sales. Special discounts are available on quantity purchases by corporations, associations, and others. For details, contact the "Special Sales Department" at the Berrett-Koehler address above.

Individual sales. Berrett-Koehler publications are available through most bookstores. They can also be ordered direct from Berrett-Koehler: Tel: (800) 929-2929; Fax: (802) 864-7626; www.bkconnection.com

Orders for college textbook/course adoption use. Please contact Berrett-Koehler: Tel: (800) 929-2929; Fax: (802) 864-7626.

Orders by U.S. trade bookstores and wholesalers. Please contact Ingram Publisher Services, Tel: (800) 509-4887; Fax: (800) 838-1149; E-mail: customer.service@ ingrampublisherservices.com; or visit www.ingrampublisherservices.com/Ordering for details about electronic ordering.

Berrett-Koehler and the BK logo are registered trademarks of Berrett-Koehler Publishers, Inc.

Printed in the United States of America

Berrett-Koehler books are printed on long-lasting acid-free paper. When it is available, we choose paper that has been manufactured by environmentally responsible processes. These may include using trees grown in sustainable forests, incorporating recycled paper, minimizing chlorine in bleaching, or recycling the energy produced at the paper mill.

Library of Congress Cataloging-in-Publication Data
Pattakos, Alex.
  Prisoners of our thoughts : Viktor Frankl's principles for discovering meaning in life and work / Alex Pattakos.—2nd ed., rev. and updated.
     p. cm.
  Includes bibliographical references and index.
  ISBN 978-1-60509-524-0 (pbk. : alk. paper)
  1. Frankl, Viktor E. (Viktor Emil), 1905-1997.   2. Logotherapy.   3. Meaning (Psychology)   4. Conduct of life.   I. Title.
  RC489.L6P38 2010
  616.89'14—dc22   2010005819

SECOND EDITION

14 13 12 11 10   10 9 8 7 6 5 4 3 2 1

Text design: Detta Penna   Cover design: Barbara Haines
Copyeditor: Sandra Craig   Cover image: ©iStockphoto.com/Sascha Burkard
Proofreader: Katherine Lee
Indexer: Kirsten Kite

Contents

Why do some people seem to have an easier time dealing with complex and challenging situations than others? Why do some people seem more capable of dealing with change than others?

Applying the therapeutic system of
world-renowned psychiatrist and philosopher
Viktor E. Frankl, learn how to bring
personal meaning and fulfillment to your everyday life and
work and to achieve your highest potential!

Core Principles

❶ *Exercise the freedom to choose your attitude.* In all situations, no matter how desperate they may appear or actually be, you always have the ultimate freedom to choose your attitude.

❷ *Realize your will to meaning.* Commit authentically to meaningful values and goals that only you can actualize and fulfill.

❸ *Detect the meaning of life's moments.* Only you can answer for your own life by detecting the meaning at any given moment and assuming responsibility for weaving your unique tapestry of existence.

❹ *Don't work against yourself.* Avoid becoming so fixated on an intent or outcome that you actually work against the desired result.

❺ *Look at yourself from a distance.* Only human beings possess the capacity to look at themselves from a distance, with a sense of perspective, including the uniquely human trait known as your sense of humor.

❻ *Shift your focus of attention.* Deflect your attention from the problem situation to something else and build your coping mechanisms for dealing with stress and change.

❼ *Extend beyond yourself.* Manifest the human spirit at work by directing your attention and relating to something more than yourself.

Prisoners of Our Thoughts

Foreword

Stephen R. Covey

Shortly before Viktor Frankl's passing in September 1997, I had heard of his declining health, illness, and hospitalization. I was very anxious to talk with him so that I could express my profound gratitude for his life's work—for his impact on millions of people, including my own life and life's work. I understood that he had lost his sight and that his wife was reading to him several hours each day in the hospital. I will never forget the feeling of hearing his voice and visiting with him. He was so kind and gracious as he listened to my expressions of appreciation, esteem, and love. I felt as if I were speaking to a great and noble spirit. After patiently listening, he said, "Stephen, you talk to me as if I am ready to check out. I still have two important projects I need to complete." How true to form! How true to character! How true to the principles of Logotherapy!

Frankl's desire and determination to continue to contribute reminded me of his collaborative work with Dr. Hans Selye of Montreal, Canada—famous for his research and writings on stress. Selye taught that it is only when we have meaningful work and projects that our immune system is strengthened and the degenerative aging forces are slowed down. He called this kind of stress "eustress" rather than distress, which comes from a life without meaning and integrity. I'm sure these two souls influenced each other, reinforcing both the physical and psychological benefits of Logotherapy, of man's search for meaning.

When Alex Pattakos graciously invited me to write a foreword to *Prisoners of Our Thoughts* and told me that the Frankl family had suggested this to him, I was both honored and excited to participate—particularly since they felt my work with organizations in management and leadership beautifully paralleled Viktor Frankl's "principles at work," the heart of this splendid book. My sense of the significance of this book deepened further when Pattakos wrote me, "A year before he died, I was sitting with Dr. Frankl in his study and he grabbed my arm and said, 'Alex, yours is the book that needs to be written!'"

I will never forget how deeply moved and inspired I was in the sixties when I studied *Man's Search for Meaning* and also *The Doctor and the Soul*. These two books, along with Frankl's other writings and lectures, reaffirmed my "soul's code" regarding our power of choice, our unique endowment of self-awareness, and our essence, our will for meaning. While on a writing sabbatical in Hawaii and in a very reflective state of mind, I was wandering through the stacks of a university library and picked up a book. I read the following three lines, which literally staggered me and again reaffirmed Frankl's essential teachings:

> Between stimulus and response, there is a space.
> In that space lies our freedom and our power to choose our
> response.
> In our response lies our growth and our happiness.

I did not note the name of the author, so I've never been able to give proper attribution. On a later trip to Hawaii I even went back to find the source and found the library building itself was no longer present.

The space between what happens to us and our response, our freedom to choose that response and the impact it can have upon our lives, beautifully illustrate that we can become a product of our decisions, not our conditions. They illustrate the three values that Frankl continually taught: the creative value, the experiential value, and the attitudinal value. We have the power to choose our response to our circumstances. We have the power to shape our circumstances; indeed, we have the responsibility, and if we ignore this space, this freedom, this responsibility, the essence of our life and our legacy could be frustrated.

One time I was leaving a military base where I had been teaching principle-centered leadership over a period of time. As I was saying good-bye to the commander of that base, a colonel, I asked him, "Why would you undertake such a significant change effort to bring principle-centered living and leadership to your command when you know full well you will be swimming upstream against powerful cultural forces? You are in your thirtieth year and you are retiring at the end of this year. You have had a successful military career and you could simply maintain the successful pattern you've had and go into your retirement with all of the honors and the plaudits that come with your dedicated years of service." His answer was unforgettable. It seared itself into my soul. He said, "Recently, my father passed away. Knowing that he was dying, he called my mother and myself to his bedside. He motioned to me to come close to him so that he could whisper something in my ear. My mother stood by, watching in tears. My father said, 'Son, promise me you won't do life like I did. Son, I didn't do right by you or by your mother, and I never really made a difference. Son, promise me you won't do life like I did.'"

This military commander said, "Stephen, that is why I am undertaking this change effort. That is why I want to bring our whole command to an entirely new level of performance and contribution. I want to make a difference, and for the first time I sincerely hope that my successors do better than I have. Up to this point, I had hoped that I would be the high-water mark, but no longer. I want to get these principles so institutionalized and so built into our culture that they will be sustainable and go on and on. I know it will be a struggle. I may even ask for an extension so that I can continue to see this work through, but I want to honor the greatest legacy that my father ever gave me, and that is the desire to make a difference."

From this commander we learn that courage is not the absence of fear but the awareness there is something more important. We spend at least a third of our life either preparing for work or doing work, usually inside organizations. Even our retirement should be filled with meaningful projects, inside organizations or families or societies. Work and love essentially comprise the essence of mortality.

The great humanistic psychologist Abraham Maslow came to similar thoughts near the end of his life, which essentially affirmed Frankl's "will to meaning" theme. He felt that his own need hierarchy theory was too needs-determined and that self-actualization was not the highest need. In the end, he concluded that self-transcendence was the human soul's highest need, which reflected more the spirit of Frankl. Maslow's wife, Bertha, and his research associate put together his final thinking along these lines in the book *The Farther Reaches of Human Nature*.

My own work with organizations and with people in the world of work focuses a great deal on developing personal and organizational mission statements. I have found that when you get enough people interacting freely and synergistically, and when these people are informed about the realities of their industry or profession and their own culture, they begin to tap into a kind of collective conscience and awareness of the need to add value, to really leave a legacy, and they set up value guidelines to fulfill that legacy. Ends and means are inseparable; in fact, the ends preexist in the means. No worthy end can ever really be accomplished with unworthy means.

I have found in my teaching that the single most exhilarating, thrilling, and motivating idea that people have ever really seriously contemplated is the idea of the power of choice—the idea that the best way to predict their future is to create it. It is basically the idea of personal freedom, of learning to ask Viktor Frankl's question: What is life asking of me? What is this situation asking of me? It's more freedom *to* rather than freedom *from*. It's definitely an inside-out rather than an outside-in approach.

I have found that when people get caught up in this awareness, this kind of mindfulness, and if they genuinely ask such questions and consult their conscience, almost always the purposes and values they come up with are transcendent—that is, they deal with meaning that is larger than their own life, one that truly adds value and contributes to other people's lives—the kinds of things that Viktor

Frankl did in the death camps of Nazi Germany. They break cycles; they establish new cycles, new positive energies. They become what I like to call "transition figures"—people who break with past cultural mindless patterns of behavior and attitude.

> The range of what we see and do
> Is limited by what we fail to notice.
> And because we fail to notice
> That we fail to notice,
> There is little we can do
> To change
> Until we notice
> How failing to notice
> Shapes our thoughts and deeds.
>
> R. D. Laing

With this kind of thinking and with the seven magnificent principles Dr. Pattakos describes in this important book, a kind of primary greatness is developed where character and contribution, conscience and love, choice and meaning, all have their play and synergy with each other. This is contrasted with secondary greatness, described in the last chapter of this book—being those who are successful in society's eyes but personally unfulfilled.

Finally, let me suggest two ideas on how to get the very most from this book. First, share or teach the core principles, one by one, to those you live with and work around who might be interested. Second, live them. To learn something but not to do is really not to learn. To know something but not to do is really not to know. Otherwise, if we just intellectualize these core principles and verbalize them but do not share and practice them, we would be like a person who is blind from birth explaining to another person what it means to see, based on an academic study of light, its properties, the eye and its anatomy. As you read this book, I challenge you to experience the freedom to choose your own attitude, to exercise your will to meaning, to detect the meaning of life's moments, to not work against yourself, to look at yourself from a distance, and to shift your focus of attention and extend beyond yourself. I suggest you consider learning this material sequentially, by reading the first principle, teaching it and applying it, then reading the next one, and so forth. You may want to simply read the entire book all at once to give yourself the overview, and then go back and learn the principles sequentially through your own experiencing. You will become a change catalyst. You will become a transition figure. You will stop bad cycles and start good ones. Life will take on a meaning as you've never known it before. I know this is so from my own experiences and from working with countless organizations and individuals in the world of work.

As my grandfather taught me, and as Viktor Frankl taught me, life is a mission, not a career.

This book is dedicated to
Viktor E. Frankl, MD, PhD (1905–1997),
whose life and legacy will forever bring light to darkness,
and
to my partner in the search for meaning and spouse,
Elaine, whose love and support will forever
bring warmth to the meaning of life.

Preface to the
Second Edition

Soon after the initial release of *Prisoners of Our Thoughts*, a massive earthquake under the Indian Ocean triggered one of the deadliest natural disasters in recorded history, known around the world as the Asian Tsunami. This tsunami killed 230,000 people and left 500,000 people homeless. Indonesia's Aceh province was closest to the epicenter of the quake and was hardest hit by the monster waves.

By chance, *Prisoners of Our Thoughts* found its way into the hands of representatives from the Jakarta-based professional services firm Dunamis Organization Services. The company developed a Volunteers' Readiness Program to prepare individuals for what they would encounter while working in Aceh. The goal was to teach the volunteers not only how to respond quickly and effectively to the vast devastation and suffering they would encounter in the field but also how to deal with their own psychological reactions. This program, which included my book as a training resource, was also employed by other organizations, including local government bodies and nongovernmental organizations such as UNESCO and UNICEF. All seven principles described in *Prisoners of Our Thoughts* were viewed as essential knowledge, skills, and attitudes required by the volunteer aid workers participating in the program.

This application of the principles in *Prisoners of Our Thoughts* alone made the book's publication worthwhile — and yes, meaningful — to me in ways I cannot adequately express. This was not an illustration of the principles in action I had envisioned when I conceptualized and wrote the book. Far from it! But since the book's publication, I have learned that its application potential is unlimited, extending far beyond the realm of work and the workplace.

Not Just for Disasters

However, the book has applications much closer to the homes and lives of most of us. Have you ever worked in a job you didn't like? Or have you felt the job was OK but you didn't feel fulfilled by the work you were doing? More broadly, have you ever wondered if there was more to life than what you were experiencing? Have you felt that bad things just happened to you, that your life was out of your control, and there was nothing you could do about it? If you answered yes to any of these questions, or even asked yourself such questions before, you are not alone. Moreover, it is natural to ask such fundamental questions about the way we live and work.

This book deals with the human quest for meaning and therefore was written with you in mind. It is grounded in the philosophy and approach of the world-renowned psychiatrist Viktor Frankl, author of *Man's Search for Meaning*, which was named one of the ten most influential books in America by the Library of Congress. Frankl, a survivor of Nazi concentration camps during World War II, is the founder of Logotherapy, a meaning-centered, humanistic approach to psychotherapy. His ideas about the search for meaning, illustrated by his own experiences and those of his clients, have influenced millions of people around the world. In this book you will find a conceptual foundation as well as practical guidance for examining your own questions about meaning in both your work and your personal life.

The particular goal of this book, though, is to bring meaning to work — that is, to do for the domain of work what Frankl did for psychotherapy. Because I define *work* very broadly, the message in this book applies to a broad audience: to volunteers as well as paid workers; to people working in all sectors and industries; to retirees; to individuals beginning a job search or career; and to those in transition. And because the book demonstrates how Frankl's principles work in a general context, the principles can be applied to life outside the workplace too. Examples, stories, exercises, questions, challenges, and other practical tools help guide you in applying Frankl's ideas about life and living to find your own path to meaning at work and in your personal life.

Frankl and Me

Frankl's influence on my work and personal life goes back almost forty years. I spent many of these years studying his groundbreaking work in existential analysis, Logotherapy, and the search for meaning, and I have applied his principles in many different work environments and situations. As a mental health professional, my reliance on the power of Frankl's ideas has evolved and expanded over time as I have tested elements of his philosophy and approach in a wide variety of organizational settings. I have also worked with many individuals who were experiencing existential dilemmas at work or in their personal lives. During this time I naturally also reflected on my own life journey and frequently relied on and benefited from Frankl's wisdom.

It is important to underscore that Viktor Frankl practiced what he preached, living and working with meaning throughout his life. This is not always easy to do, as I know from personal experience. There is a saying in the academic world that we don't know what we don't know until we try to teach it. The same thing can be said about writing a book. And yet in many respects, *writing* a book is the easy part. The really hard part, I must confess, comes when we try to *do* what we write about. I can only try to follow Frankl's lead.

It was in a meeting with Frankl at his home in Vienna in 1996 when I first proposed the idea of writing a book that would apply his core principles and approach explicitly to work and the workplace—to the world of business. Frankl was more than encouraging—in his typical passionate style, he leaned across his desk, grabbed my arm, and said "Alex, yours is the book that needs to be written." I felt that Frankl's words burned into the core of my being, and I was determined from that moment to make this book idea a reality.

I realize now more than ever the good fortune and benefit I have had of metaphorically standing on the shoulders of Viktor Frankl, one of the greatest thinkers of modern times. Through his own story of finding a reason to live in the horrendous circumstances of Nazi concentration camps, Dr. Frankl has left a legacy that can help everyone, no matter what their situation, find deeper, richer meaning in their lives. It is my intention and hope that *Prisoners of Our Thoughts* not only builds upon Frankl's legacy of meaning in

life and work but also supports and advances his legacy so it
is never forgotten.

Welcome to the Second Edition

New and updated stories, new applications and exercises, and
a new chapter 12, The Meaning Difference®, offer rich testimony to support the broad—even global—appeal of the
search for meaning in society today. This book delivers a life-
affirming, inspirational message that is especially needed in
our fast-changing, increasingly complex, and uncertain world.
My experience in helping to deliver this meaning-centered
message has underscored the vital importance of this need,
and at the same time, it has been a source of personal growth.
As an author, I am honored and humbled to have such an
opportunity to practice what I preach. At the same time, I
recognize that this kind of opportunity can also be quite a
challenge—it is always easier to advise others to do what I
say, not what I *do!*

　　After you read this book, I challenge you not to put
it away, out of your sight and mind. Please don't do that,

because the core principles I've distilled from Frankl's voluminous work deserve more of your attention than a simple read-through will provide. I would like you to live this book by practicing the exercises, reviewing the concepts and cases, and adopting the principles in your daily work and life. Only in this way will the book be more than just another volume in your library. Only in this way can the book help you to find true meaning in your work and life. And only in this way will the message Frankl branded on my soul — "Alex, yours is the book that needs to be written!" — have the kind of meaning he intended.

Alex Pattakos, PhD
Santa Fe, New Mexico, USA
March 2010

Life Doesn't Just Happen to Us

Ultimately, man should not ask what the meaning of his life is, but rather must recognize that it is he who is asked. In a word, each man is questioned by life; and he can only answer to life by answering for his own life; to life he can only respond by being responsible.[1]

Every day Vita delivers my mail — cheerfully. It's her trademark attitude. One day, in lousy weather, I heard her whistling as she went about making her deliveries. Instinctively I shouted out to her, "Thank you for doing such a great job." She stopped dead in her tracks with surprise. "Thank you," she said. "Wow, I'm not accustomed to hearing such words. I really appreciate it."

I wanted to know more. "How do you stay so positive and upbeat about delivering mail every day?" I asked her.

"I don't just deliver mail," she said. "I see myself helping to connect people to other people. I help build the community. Besides, people depend on me and I don't want to let them down." Her response was enthusiastic and proud.

Vita's attitude about her work reflected the words inscribed on the General Post Office building in New York

City: "Neither snow nor rain nor gloom of night stays these couriers from the swift completion of their appointed rounds." The Greek historian Herodotus wrote these words in the fifth century BC. The ancient delivery of messages from one person to another is at the very heart of our Information Age, yet these days it's the phrase "going postal" that we're more likely to recognize.

Fair or unfair, "going postal" has become the symbol of all the negativity a job has to offer: boredom, repetitiveness, exposure to the elements, dangerous dogs, irritated customers, and a kind of automated behavior that ultimately inspires an explosion of pent-up rage—a killing spree, retaliation against all the suffered injustice of the job.

> What threatens contemporary man is the alleged meaninglessness of his life, or, as I call it, the existential vacuum within him. And when does this vacuum open up, when does this so often latent vacuum become manifest? In the state of boredom.[2]

No matter what our opinions might be about the stature of any career or profession, it is the person doing the job that gives the job meaning. Vita is proof that those ancient words of Herodotus are alive and well in the twenty-first century.

But Vita's attitude goes beyond the "swift completion of her appointed rounds" (to paraphrase Herodotus). She experiences her work as serving a higher purpose. Her attitude about her job and its drudgery goes far beyond an exercise in positive thinking. Vita sees her mail delivery responsibility as a personal, life-saving mission, one that could be fulfilled only by her. She knows she is depended on, perhaps even by people who feel disdain for her work, and it means something. She brings meaning to her job, and in turn, her work becomes meaningful.

I am convinced that, in the final analysis, there is no situation that does not contain within it the seed of a meaning.[3]

Why is it that some people, like Vita my mail carrier, experience their work—even mundane work—with passion and commitment? Why do some people have an easier time dealing with complex and challenging situations at work and in life? Why do some people deal more easily with change? Why do some people find meaning and fulfillment in their work and everyday life, while others do not? There are no simple answers to these complex questions; but there are meaningful answers. That is the goal of this book: to illuminate the search for meaning as a path to meaning, both in our work and in our lives outside work.

This Book Is About True Freedom

We are by nature creatures of habit. Searching for a life that is both predictable and within our comfort zone, we rely on routine and, for the most part, learned thinking patterns. In effect, we create pathways in our minds in much the same way that a path is beaten through a grass field from repeated use. And because these patterns are automatic, we may believe these habitual ways of thinking and behaving to be beyond our control. Life, it seems, just happens to us. Not only do we rationalize our responses to life but we also fall prey to forces that limit our potential as human beings. By viewing ourselves as relatively powerless and driven by our instincts, the possibility that we create, or at least cocreate, our own reality becomes difficult to grasp. Instead, we lock ourselves inside our own mental prisons. We lose sight of our own natural potential and that of others.

Each of us has his own inner concentration camp . . . we must deal with, with forgiveness and patience—as full human beings; as we are and what we will become.[4]

The ways in which we hold ourselves "prisoners of our thoughts" are well documented in the work of many writers and thinkers who explore the landscape of our psychospiritual lives. Physician Deepak Chopra, in the audiotape of his book *Unconditional Life*, says "We erect and build a prison, and the tragedy is that we cannot even see the walls of this prison."[5]

Yet we can reshape our patterns of thinking. Through our own search for meaning, we can unfreeze ourselves from our limited perspective, find the key, and unlock the door of our metaphorical prison cell.

Viktor Frankl, a psychiatrist who suffered through imprisonment in Nazi concentration camps during World War II, found meaning in spite of—and because of—the suffering all around him. His life's work resulted in the therapeutic approach called *Logotherapy*, which paved the way for us to know meaning as a foundation of our existence. Frankl is quick to say, however, that such traumatic suffering is *not* a prerequisite for finding meaning in our lives. He means that whenever we suffer—no matter what the severity of our suffering is—we have the ability to find meaning in the situation. Choosing to do so is the path to a meaningful life.

This book explores seven core principles that I have derived from Frankl's voluminous body of work:

1. We are free to choose our attitude toward everything that happens to us.

2. We can realize our will to meaning by making a conscious, authentic commitment to meaningful values and goals.

3. We can find meaning in all of life's moments.

4. We can learn to see how we work against ourselves and can learn to avoid thwarting our intentions.

5. We can look at ourselves from a distance to gain insight and perspective as well as to laugh at ourselves.

6. We can shift our focus of attention when we are coping with difficult situations.

7. We can reach out beyond ourselves and make a difference in the world.

These seven principles, which I believe form the foundation of Frankl's thinking and approach, are available to us anytime, all the time. They can lead us to meaning, to freedom, and to deep connection to our own lives and to the lives of others in our local and global communities.

Viewing life as inherently meaningful and with unlimited potential requires a shift in consciousness. It also requires responsible action on our part for, as Frankl points out, the potential for meaning that exists in each moment of life can only be searched for and detected by each of us individually. This responsibility, he says, is "to be actualized by each of us at any time, even in the most miserable situations and literally up to the last breath of ourselves."[6]

Frankl walked this path completely. By living a life with meaning right to his last breath, he showed us how his philosophy and therapeutic approach were grounded in practice. His personal experiences throughout his long life, both as a survivor of the Nazi death camps and as a revered and respected thought leader, illuminate the unlimited potential of a human being. His life gives us rich and ample evidence that the keys to freedom from life's prison cells—real and imagined—are within, and within reach.

Whether we choose this path of liberation is a decision that only we as individuals can make and for which only we can be held responsible. When we search out and discover the authentic meaning of our existence and our experiences, we discover that life doesn't happen to us. We happen to life; and we make it meaningful.

Humanizing Work

A meaningful life includes meaningful work. Let's face it, most people spend at least half of their waking lives "at work" or working in some way. Yet where do most people look to find meaning in their life? The usual answer is in their *personal* life—in their relationships or their religious or spiritual practice. But what about their job? Can people find true meaning at work?

The transformation of work in the twenty-first century is, in many respects, a call for humanity—a new consciousness that suggests more than simply trying to strike a balance between our work and personal lives. It is a call to honor our individuality and fully engage our human spirit at work—wherever that may be. While this idea of empowering workers in body, mind, and spirit is not new, actually putting it to work is new. In some ways, technological advances have redesigned work to better accommodate human factors. What we need now is a way to elevate the human spirit at work and to integrate in a positive, meaningful way this spiritual dimension of work with our everyday life.

One of the goals of this book is to bring meaning to work and, quite frankly, to do for the domain of work what

Frankl as a psychiatrist was able to do for psychotherapy. His unique approach is internationally recognized as a system of humanistic psychotherapy, and Frankl himself has been referred to by some people as the founder of humanistic medicine and psychiatry as well as of existential analysis. Logotherapy, in short, seeks to make us aware of our freedom of response to all aspects of our destiny. This humanistic view of psychotherapy helps clients to find concrete meaning in their lives. As a therapeutic system, it strengthens trust in the unconditional meaningfulness of life and the dignity of the person. By applying this philosophy to work and the workplace, we can more deeply humanize our working lives and bring deeper meaning to work itself. In turn, by bringing deeper meaning to our working lives, we can more deeply humanize and enrich the meaning of our personal—that is, nonworking—lives.

From the perspective of Logotherapy, we can find unconditional meaning in our work situations and experience the unconditional value of our colleagues as unique human beings as we do with our family members and close friends. This is not an easy task, but when we celebrate our differences as cheerfully as we celebrate our similarities, the result is a powerful synergy at work and in the workplace. Best-selling author Stephen R. Covey, who has also been influenced by Frankl's teachings, has observed that "difference is the beginning of synergy."[7] When business leaders and managers on all levels bring this awareness to work, they are the catalysts for profound changes in the workplace—changes that enhance everyone's ability to search for and find meaning, on the job, at home, and within our entire human experience.

Unconditional meaning, however, is paralleled by the uncondi-
tional value of each and every person. It is that which warrants
the indelible quality of the dignity of man. Just as life remains
potentially meaningful under any conditions, even those which
are most miserable, so too does the value of each and every person
stay with him or her.[8]

Detecting Your Path

Of course, being fully human and living an authentic life at home, at play, and at work are formidable challenges. They involve a willingness to embark down a path of self-discovery, drawing heavily upon what Frankl refers to as our "will to meaning"—that is, our inherent capacity to continually search for meaning under all circumstances. This human quest for meaning in every moment creates a path of discernment that runs through all aspects of our lives. This quest, this path is of course a process, not a product, for during our lifetime there is no final destination where everything comes to rest. This book offers guideposts along the way.

In chapter 2, Viktor Frankl's Lifework and Legacy, we look briefly into the life and work of Dr. Frankl. As a mentor and author, he had a profound impact on my way of thinking and dramatically influenced my work and personal life. As the founder of Logotherapy, he brought powerful insights and compassion to the therapeutic world, leaving a legacy of wisdom that only increases over time.

The many pathways to meaning are explored in chapter 3, Labyrinths of Meaning, which also refers to the seven core principles of Frankl's work introduced earlier. Each of these life-meaning principles is then more deeply explored in individual chapters: Exercise the Freedom to Choose Your Attitude (chapter 4), Realize Your Will to Meaning (chapter 5), Detect the Meaning of Life's Moments (chapter 6), Don't Work Against Yourself (chapter 7), Look at Yourself from a Distance (chapter 8), Shift Your Focus of Attention (chapter 9), and Extend Beyond Yourself (chapter 10).

One may say that instincts are transmitted through the genes, and values are transmitted through traditions, but that meanings, being unique, are a matter of personal discovery.[9]

Chapter 4, Exercise the Freedom to Choose Your Attitude, examines the logotherapeutic concept of freedom of will. This concept is best described by Frankl's famous quote in *Man's Search for Meaning*, "Everything can be taken from a man but...the last of the human freedoms—to choose one's attitude in any given set of circumstances, to choose one's way."[10] The key ingredient here is the responsibility for choosing our attitude, which lies solely and soundly with the self.

Chapter 5, Realize Your Will to Meaning, explores Frankl's concept of our will to meaning and how we bring our values to life at work. Logotherapy, according to Frankl, "considers man as a being whose main concern consists of fulfilling a meaning and in actualizing *values*, rather than in the mere gratification and satisfaction of drives and instincts."[11] Giving meaning to work, in this context, means more than simply completing a task to receive a tangible reward, such as money, influence, status, or prestige. By committing to values and goals that might appear intangible but are nonetheless real and meaningful, we honor our deepest needs, just as we seek to do in our personal lives.

The fundamental presumption is that only as individuals can we answer for our own lives, detecting in them each moment's meaning and weaving our own unique tapestry of existence. Chapter 6, Detect the Meaning of Life's Moments, goes farther—into the realm of ultimate meaning, or super-meaning. Frankl's holistic views on the importance of our intuitive capacity for love and conscience offer great insight into how meaning reveals itself in everyday life and at work. Frankl has written: "Love is the ultimate and the highest goal to which man can aspire.... The salvation of man is through love and in love."[12] Yet our ability to weave love into our lives, especially into our work lives, is not only sadly limited but also suspect in today's measurable and impersonal world of work.

Sometimes our most fervent desires and intentions are thwarted by our obsession with outcomes. In chapter 7, Don't Work Against Yourself, the technique known as *paradoxical intention* is examined and applied to work and everyday life situations. Frankl calls this form of self-sabotage *hyperinten-tion*. The tendency to micromanage the work of others, for example, may create hyperintensive stress, performance anxi-ety, or even covert or overt actions of sabotage that can end up creating the opposite of the result sought by a manager. (A similar result also has been observed in cases where well-meaning parents, under the guise of parental guidance, try to micromanage their teenagers, who are predisposed to being contrarian!) Sometimes focusing too closely on a problem can keep us from seeing the solution. Likewise, becoming fix-ated on a particular outcome often gets in the way of our best intentions.

Chapter 8, Look at Yourself from a Distance, focuses on the notion of self-detachment and how, among other things, it can help us to lighten up and not sweat the small stuff. Frankl observed, "Only man owns the capacity to detach himself from himself. To look at himself out of some perspective or distance."[13] This capacity includes that uniquely human trait known as a sense of humor. Frankl noted that "no animal is capable of laughing, least of all laughing *at itself* or *about itself*."[14] A dose of self-detachment frees us to be more receptive to the universe of opportunities in our lives.

When Viktor Frankl was a prisoner in the Nazi concentration camps, in order to cope with stress, suffering, and conflict, he learned to deflect his attention away from the painful situation to other, more appealing circumstances. In chapter 9, Shift Your Focus of Attention, we explore this skill and how it can be effectively used in the workplace and outside work.

Self-transcendence is explored in chapter 10, Extend Beyond Yourself. This principle goes far beyond shifting the focus of attention from one thing to another. It takes us into the spiritual realm of ultimate meaning, where we see how our lives connect seamlessly to the lives of others. We see how being of service, no matter what the scale, is where our deepest meaning is realized. And we learn how to effectively manifest the human spirit in our personal and work lives by relating and being directed to something greater than ourselves.

In chapter 11, Living and Working with Meaning, I weave my own views into Frankl's lessons so that they can be integrated into daily work and life, bringing personal and ultimate meaning to all the moments of our lives. In this connection, I use one of Frankl's methods of meaning analysis as a frame of reference for examining the extent to which our lives, including our work lives, are focused on meaning.

Finally, chapter 12, The Meaning Difference®, summarizes both qualitative and quantitative research demonstrating the critical role of meaning in improving the quality of people's lives, increasing happiness, and promoting health and wellness. The links between a personal sense of meaning and happiness, resilience, engagement, and health are examined, and the determining influence of the human quest for meaning on these quality-of-life factors is underscored for its existential value. Here we also get a glimpse at what trends related to the search for meaning loom on the horizon and what they portend for the future of the human race.

So, let's first take a look at Dr. Frankl's lifework, explore more fully the foundations of his meaning-centered approach, and see how we can apply his groundbreaking philosophy to work, workplace issues, and our personal lives.

Meaning Moment Recall a situation in which you felt especially negative about your job or career. Perhaps you just didn't like the work you were doing, or maybe you disliked your supervisor, boss, or co-workers (this may even be your situation today). Alternatively, recall a situation in your personal life, such as a relationship or family matter, about which you felt especially negative. Did you view yourself as a victim of circumstances that were outside your control, or did you feel responsible in some way for creating the situation and therefore feel ultimately responsible for dealing with it? What, if anything, did you do about it? As you think about the situation now, what did you learn from it? What could you have done differently?

Prisoners of Our Thoughts

Meaning Question: What can you do to make your life or your current work/job more meaningful?

FOR FURTHER
REFLECTION

Ask yourself honestly, Am I a prisoner of my thoughts? Do I hold other people, including co-workers, family members, or friends, prisoners of my thoughts?

Viktor Frankl's
Lifework and Legacy

*I do not forget any good deed done to me,
and I carry no grudge for a bad one.*[15]

It seems that I have known Viktor Frankl most of my life. It was in the late 1960s when I first became acquainted with his work and read his now-classic book *Man's Search for Meaning*. While on active duty with the U.S. Army, I received formal training at Brooke Army Hospital (now called Brooke Army Medical Center) at Fort Sam Houston in San Antonio, Texas, as a social work/psychology specialist. In addition to the opportunity to work side by side with some of the best mental health professionals in the field, this unique learning experience fueled my passion for studying various schools of thought and practice in psychiatry and psychology. Frankl's work in particular had great resonance for me at that time, and it eventually became an integral part of both my personal and professional life.

Over the years, in fact, I have had many opportunities to

apply Frankl's teachings in my own life and work. In effect, I have been able to field test the validity and reliability of his key principles and techniques, often in comparison with competing schools of thought and in situations that tested the limits of my personal resilience. It didn't take me long to realize the efficacy of his philosophy and approach, and I became a de facto practitioner of Logotherapy long before the idea for this book surfaced in my mind.

Many decisive times in my life, including situations that involved my work or employment, could easily be described as turbulent and challenging. Such formidable, life-defining moments (although they often lasted much longer than a moment!) required a great deal of soul-searching for answers. I remember how truly out of balance—and yes, even lost—I felt at those critical times in my life. Parenthetically, I learned not many years ago from Thomas Moore, psychotherapist and author of the best-selling book *Care of the Soul*, that our most soulful times are when we are out of balance rather than when we are in balance! In any event, it was especially during these meaning-centered moments that I found myself putting Frankl's philosophy and approach into practice.

Let me now share a work-related example that tested my personal resilience and how I applied some of Frankl's core principles to deal with the situation in a responsible manner. This life-defining situation involved my full-time, albeit summer, employment with a large engineering and construction firm in New Jersey. I had recently graduated from college and was contemplating going to law school after my military service. With the help and urging of my father, I took a job with the contract administration department at this company with the expectation that it would provide some useful legal experience and assist in my decision to pursue a career in law. My father, who was an engineer by profession, envisioned that some day I would work for him and his company as an attorney specializing in contract law.

This type of career path, I should note, was a far cry from what I had envisioned for myself—I did not see myself as a corporate attorney. The only interest that I had in law at the time was how it could be used as an instrument for social policy and societal change. Such a perspective, especially during the Vietnam War era, did not bode well for my relationship with my father and my employer. In short, I felt trapped and believed I needed to resolve the situation quickly if I was going to survive the summer. Freedom in my sights, I began to plan my escape. My father had always been an authoritative figure in my life, but I was keenly aware of course that my particular situation, no matter how unbearable and confining it seemed to be at the time, could never be compared to imprisonment in the Nazi death camps! Again, I want to stress that in no way do I mean to make light of this comparison.

I have Frankl to thank for helping me assess my situation and then choose my response to it. First, I decided up front that I would maintain a positive attitude toward the situation, especially since I had faith in my ability to orchestrate an eventual escape from my perceived predicament. Second, in no uncertain terms, the situation presented me with an opportunity to clarify and confirm my values about the kind of work that I wanted to do and *not* do. To use Dr. Frankl's words, I was determined to realize my will to meaning and only do work that was aligned with my core values.

Third, during the short time that I was employed by this company, I was able consciously to practice the Logotherapy principles of *de-reflection* (shifting my focus of attention onto things that mattered to me) and *self-detachment* (maintaining a sense of humor). Fourth, my experience at the company and in my particular job assignment helped me to identify and weave together the various strands of meaning that seemed most important to me—both in terms of the kind of work that I wanted to do and the kind of life that I wanted to live. Even though it meant standing up to and engaging in many heated arguments with my father so that I could declare the path that *I* wanted to pursue, I learned from this situation that it was worth the risk and effort!

In the end, my passion to realize my will to meaning resulted in straining the relationship with my father, quitting my job, and changing my academic program objectives. In hindsight, however, the way that I chose to handle this particular situation—clearly a life-defining moment for a still relatively immature twenty-something—also increased my personal resilience for handling similar challenges in the future.

As you have gathered, Frankl's thinking has profoundly influenced my life and work paths over the years. I've also had the great privilege of meeting Dr. Frankl personally and seeking his counsel. This book, in fact, is a product of his guiding influence and personal encouragement.

A Life with Meaning

Viktor Frankl's calling came early. Long before the Holocaust took its horrific toll and became the ground from which sprang his most influential book, *Man's Search for Meaning*, Frankl's own search for meaning was already underway. At the tender age of sixteen, he gave his first public lecture, "On the Meaning of Life." Two years later, for his high school graduation essay, he wrote "On the Psychology of Philosophical Thought." It was almost as though on some level he was preparing for the tragedy that lay in his future and the role he would play in giving hope to all of humankind after the hopelessness and despair of the Holocaust. At a young age, Frankl had become convinced that the human spirit is what makes us unique and that reducing life and human nature to "nothing but," along the lines of many existentialist philosophers and psychiatrists of his time, denied or discounted any such spirit.

However, it was not until he went through the hell of despair over the apparent meaninglessness of life—and struggled with the pessimism associated with such a reductionist and ultimately nihilistic view of life—that he was able to develop his therapeutic system of Logotherapy. At a conference in San Diego in 1980, Frankl said that he had wrestled with this view that undercut faith in life's meaning, like Jacob with the angel did, until he could "say yes to life in spite of everything." Interestingly, an earlier version of *Man's Search for Meaning* had this very quotation as its title.

Frankl was born in Vienna, Austria, on March 26, 1905. It was the day Beethoven died, and in his autobiography, he is quick to note this coincidence and reveal his sense of humor by sharing a comment made by one of his schoolmates: "One mishap comes seldom alone."[16] His father, who had been forced to drop out of medical school for financial reasons, was a public servant who instilled in the young Viktor a Spartan rationality along with a firm sense of social justice.

For thirty-five years, Viktor's father had worked for the department of child protection and youth welfare. His mother, with whom he was very close, helped him develop his emotional side—the feelings and human connectedness that would inform his work as deeply as did his rationality.

He was the second of three children and at an early age was afflicted with perfectionism. "I do not even speak to myself for days," he said, referring to his anger at himself for not always being perfect. His astonishing and precocious interests led him to write to Sigmund Freud, with whom he had a correspondence throughout his high school years. It was a correspondence lost to Gestapo destruction years later, when Frankl was deported to the concentration camps.

In 1924, at Freud's request, Frankl published his first article in the *International Journal of Psychoanalysis*. He was nineteen years old and had already developed two of his fundamental ideas: First, that we ourselves must answer the question that life asks us about the meaning of our lives, and that we ourselves are responsible for our existence. Second, that ultimate meaning is beyond our comprehension and must remain so—we must have faith in it as we pursue it. These ideas were the basis for his observations during the years of his Nazi imprisonment. They survived the darkest tests imaginable and, in fact, grew in strength for Frankl even as they were most challenged.

In 1924 he also started medical studies, and his growing professional recognition included a developing relationship with the renowned psychiatrist Alfred Adler. It was Adler who invited him to publish another article, this time in the *International Journal of Individual Psychology*. Frankl still was only twenty years old.

A year later, during public lectures in Germany, Frankl used the word *Logotherapy* for the first time. Frankl was not drawn to the dehumanizing and reductionist nature of psychotherapy. His work acknowledged human weakness but it went further, to acknowledge the underlying meaning behind weakness and the potential we all have to learn from and transform our weaknesses. "I am convinced," he said, "that, in the final analysis, there is no situation that does not contain within it the seed of a meaning."[17] This belief of an idealistic young man became the foundation of Logotherapy, which continues today to inform and inspire our human struggle to search for and find meaning in our lives.

But, as in most scientific disciplines, Frankl's was not a simple, unchallenged path. By the time he received his medical degree in 1930, he was banished from the Adler circle because he chose to support an alternative point of view. He had already gained an international reputation for his work in youth counseling, however, and from 1930 to 1938 was on the staff of the psychiatric University Clinic in Vienna. When in 1938 the Germans invaded Austria, he had an established private practice in neurology and psychiatry.

During the early part of the war, Frankl and his family were afforded a measure of protection because of his position as chief of the neurological department at Rothschild Hospital, the only Jewish hospital in Vienna. He risked his life and saved the lives of others by sabotaging, through the use of false diagnoses, the Nazi procedures requiring the euthanasia of mentally ill patients. It was during this time that he started writing his first book, *The Doctor and the Soul*, later to be confiscated by the Nazis.

In September 1942, Frankl and his family were arrested

and deported to the Theresienstadt concentration camp near Prague. This was the beginning of three dark years of imprisonment during which Frankl lost his wife, Tilly, his parents, and his brother to the horrors of the Nazi prison camps. He was incarcerated at Auschwitz-Birkenau, Dachau, and finally, at Türkheim, where he nearly died from typhoid fever and kept himself going by reconstructing his manuscript on bits of paper stolen from the camp office. In his autobiography, Frankl recollected, "I am convinced that I owe my survival, among other things, to my resolve to reconstruct that lost manuscript."[18]

In his book *Man's Search for Meaning*, Frankl writes about his experiences in the concentration camps. He writes graphically and unflinchingly about the treatment, torture, and murder of the prisoners. He also writes about the beauty of the human spirit—how it could transcend the horror and find meaning under the most unimaginable circumstances. Frankl's experiences and observations reinforced the principles of meaning he had developed in his youth. At the end of the war, as a survivor and as a psychiatrist, he knew that his theories of Logotherapy had greater authenticity and ever deeper meaning. He wrote about the ongoing nightmares resulting from his experiences, but he also knew those experiences laid the groundwork for his belief in self-transcendence and the will to meaning:

> *I can see beyond the misery of the situation to the potential for discovering a meaning behind it, and thus to turn an apparently meaningless suffering into a genuine human achievement. I am convinced that, in the final analysis, there is no situation that does not contain within it the seed of a meaning.*[19]

After the war, Frankl returned to Vienna and became director of the Vienna Neurological Policlinic, a position he held for twenty-five years. He also started a long and distinguished academic career that took him to the University of Vienna, Harvard University, and many other universities throughout the world. He received twenty-nine honorary doctorates during his life and wrote thirty-two books, which have been translated into twenty-seven languages. *Man's Search for Meaning* is considered by the Library of Congress to be one of the ten most influential books in America.

In 1992 the Viktor Frankl Institute was established in Vienna. Today the institute continues to serve as the center of a worldwide network of research and training institutes and societies dedicated to advancing his philosophy and therapeutic system of Logotherapy and existential analysis. Frankl died peacefully on September 2, 1997, at the age of ninety-two. He remained creative, productive, and passionate to the end of his life. His very presence touched and helped others. Indeed, psychologist Jeffrey Zeig, who was privileged to know Frankl and his family, anchored his sentiments about the influence of Frankl in words taken from Albert Camus's *The First Man:* "There are people who vindicate the world, who help others just by their presence." Without a doubt, Viktor Frankl was a man whose presence vindicated the world.

A Legacy of Meaning

The influence of Frankl's exceptional life and work has been profound. His writing alone has had an impact on people from all walks of life — educators, students, religious leaders (including Pope Paul VI), politicians, philosophers, psychologists, psychiatrists, and millions of others in search of meaning in their lives. Yet he was a humble man, modest, and not interested in promoting himself in the fashion of the times.

He was also inspirational to those whose lives were anchored in struggle. For example, one young man from Texas, Jerry Long, seventeen years old, was the victim of a paralyzing diving accident. He was left a quadriplegic and was able to type only by using a pencil-size rod that he held in his mouth. But he remained committed to becoming a psychologist because he liked people and wanted to help them. He wrote to Frankl as a college freshman after reading *Man's Search for Meaning*, remarking that his difficulties seemed to be far less than those suffered by Frankl and his comrades. Jerry found new insights every time he read Frankl's book. He said, "I have suffered but I know that, without the suffering, the growth I have achieved would not have been possible."

When he eventually met Dr. Frankl in person, he told him, "The accident broke my back, but it did not break me."[20] Despite his severe handicap, Jerry was able to fulfill his goal of becoming a psychologist, earning his doctorate in clinical psychology in 1990. Dr. Jerry L. Long Jr., who died in 2004, was an extraordinary, inspirational figure and, as Dr. Frankl rightly observed, was a living testimony to "the defiant power of the Spirit." Besides his contributions as a practicing clinician in Logotherapy and a teacher (he held several adjunct professorships in the Dallas/Fort Worth, Texas, area), Jerry excelled as a public speaker and motivational role model. Moreover, in 1998 he contributed a piece to a journal commemorating the recently deceased Viktor Frankl, in which he included the following passage:

Once, after speaking to a large audience, I was asked if I ever felt sad because I could no longer walk. I replied, "Professor Frankl can hardly see, I cannot walk at all, and many of you can hardly cope with life. What is crucial to remember is this—we don't need just our eyes, just our legs, or just our minds. All we need are the wings of our souls and together we can fly."[21]

In Frankl's words, "You do not have to suffer to learn. But, if you don't learn from suffering, over which you have no control, then your life becomes truly meaningless.... The way in which a man accepts his fate—those things beyond his control—can add a deeper meaning to his life. He controls how he responds."[22]

In the death camps of Nazi Germany, Frankl saw men who walked through the huts comforting others, giving away their last piece of bread. "They may have been few in number," he wrote, "but they offer sufficient proof that everything can be taken from a man but one thing: the last of human freedoms—to choose one's attitude in any given set of circumstances, to choose one's own way."[23]

This statement is perhaps one of the most often quoted passages from Frankl's work. U.S. Senator John McCain attributed his own survival as a prisoner of war in Vietnam for five and a half years in large part to the learning he acquired from Frankl's experience and teachings. In fact, Senator McCain began the preface to his memoir, *Faith of My Fathers* (1999), with the same Frankl quotation.

In the field of work and meaning, references to Frankl's work are numerous. Best-selling author Stephen R. Covey, who wrote *The 7 Habits of Highly Effective People*, was particularly influenced by Frankl's vision. In their book *First Things First: To Live, to Love, to Learn, to Leave a Legacy*, Covey and his associates refer to Frankl's concentration camp experiences and cite the following passage from *Man's Search for Meaning*: "The single most important factor, he realized, was a sense of future vision—the impelling conviction of those who were to survive that they had a mission to perform, some important work left to do."[24]

Viktor Frankl leaves a profound legacy. Through his life and his work, he reminds us that we all have important work to do, that whatever we do is important, and that meaning can be found everywhere, all the time.

Meaning Moment Recall a situation in your personal life or work in which you felt trapped or confined (this may even be your situation today). Perhaps you just didn't have the freedom or authority to deal with the situation in the way that ideally you would have liked. What, if anything, did you do about it? What, in other words, was your escape plan? As you think about the situation now, what did you learn from it? In hindsight, what could you have done differently?

Meaning Question: What is your vision of the kind of work that you really want to do or kind of life that you really would like to live?

FOR FURTHER REFLECTION

Consider the hardships you have experienced in your personal and work life. How might Frankl's experience in the concentration camps help you deal with such hardships in the past, present, or future?

Prisoners of Our Thoughts

Labyrinths of Meaning

*I wish to stress that the true meaning of life is
to be discovered in the world rather than within man
or his own psyche, as though it were a closed system.*[25]

In an episode of the popular American television sitcom
Frasier, the central character, Dr. Frasier Crane, played by
Kelsey Grammer, is notified that he will receive a Lifetime
Achievement Award for his work as a psychiatrist and radio
talk show host. Prior to the award ceremonies, Frasier seeks
the counsel of his psychiatric mentor because he feels anxious and ambivalent about receiving the award. More fundamentally, however, the session with his mentor reveals that
Frasier feels empty in spite of all his professional success. At
the award ceremonies, his acceptance speech is noticeably
brief and ends with the existential question, "Now what do I
do with the rest of my life?" In this fictitious case, the concern
is very real. Frasier had reached a critical point along his life
path and couldn't see where he was going next. Walking a
labyrinth through all of its twists and turns is like this.

A labyrinth is not a maze or a puzzle to be solved but a path of meaning to be experienced. Its path is circular and convoluted but it has no dead ends. A labyrinth has one entrance—one way in and one way out. When we walk the path, we go around short curves and long curves; sometimes we are out on the edge, sometimes we circle around the center. We are never really lost, but, like Frasier, we can never quite see where we are going. Along the path we sometimes move forward with ease and confidence; sometimes we creep ahead cautiously; sometimes we find the need to stop and reflect; and sometimes we even feel the urge to retreat. The center is there but our path takes us through countless twists and turns. Sometimes we are at the heart of our life experiences, sometimes we are at a playful turn; sometimes we share our path with others, and other times we don't. No matter what, we are still on the labyrinth path. It holds all our experiences, in life and in work. And to draw upon the wisdom of the ancient Greek philosopher Heraclitus, we need to be aware that what looks like an *end* point can also be a *beginning* point. Indeed, in so many ways, the labyrinth is like life.

Many great cathedrals were built on the sites of ancient labyrinths. At Chartres Cathedral in France, the eleven-circuit labyrinth on the floor of the cathedral is considered by some as symbolic of the ancient pilgrimage to Jerusalem. But the labyrinth is also a metaphor for what is sacred in our lives. Through its twists and turns, its ancient spaciousness holds everything we experience—our minds and emotions, our physical beings and our spirits, our losses and gains, our successes and failures, our joys and sorrows. When we walk the path inward, we carry our burdens with us. When we meditate or pray in the center, we ask for grace, forgiveness, and understanding. When we walk the path outward, we are lighter, more joyful, and ready again to take on our life's challenges.

Because of my Greek family heritage, which is rooted in Crete, I've long been fascinated with the Cretan labyrinth, a classic seven-circuit labyrinth dating back more than four thousand years. Some people believe the Cretan design evolved from the spirals found throughout nature, but it's the ancient myth of Theseus entering the labyrinth at Knossos to fight the Minotaur that captured my imagination. As a child I wanted to explore the unknown; I wanted to be of service, even as I defied authority to find my way along the twists and turns of the path. And as convoluted as it sometimes was, the path has remained my own. As I reflect back, there is a harmony that I couldn't have predicted.

I encountered the work of Viktor Frankl more than thirty years ago, and although my work has changed dramatically over the years, his teachings about meaning remain the foundation of my working life. While serving on active duty with the U.S. Army in the late 1960s, I saw how the casualties of war—military and civilian—needed to find meaning in order to heal. In Chicago in the 1970s, while working in the mental health field, I saw how people with schizophrenia could find meaning and create meaningful lives without drugs, psychosurgery, or electroshock treatments. In the 1980s, I realized that linking the contradictions of business theory and practice was essential for an authentic life. In the 1990s, I began to understand that business could actually take the lead in societal and global transformation. And in the first decade of the new millennium, I observed a major shift in consciousness among people working in all sectors about what really matters in life and how that new awareness can be translated into making a positive difference for themselves and others.

The labyrinth that is my life has taken me from the personal to the theoretical and back again. Yet it is Frankl's deep belief in the inherent meaning of life that has steadily informed and inspired me, leading me deeper into my life path, deeper into authentic meaning.

Exploring Our Work Lives As Labyrinths

When we explore our work lives as labyrinths of meaning, with all of the design features of classic labyrinths noted earlier, we deepen our experience. When we see our work as expressions of our bodies, minds, and spirits, we honor our inner lives as well as our connectedness to others and to the outside world. Meaning is everywhere. This is true whether we drive a bus or run a corporation.

While attending a conference in New Orleans about a year before the devastating Hurricane Katrina, I had the opportunity to encounter and experience Winston, a chartered bus driver for attendees of major conventions. To his customers, at least initially, Winston is only a bus driver, someone who makes sure that they travel between their hotel and the convention center safely and on time. To Winston, on the other hand, his customers represent a labyrinth of experience as well as an important source of meaning at work and in his life.

"Welcome to Nawlins," Winston would say as he greeted everyone boarding his bus. In addition to pointing out what he felt were significant sights along his route, he would ask passengers if they had any questions about the city and was eager to offer *his* recommendations to enhance their experience. He would tell jokes and get everyone laughing, and he was even able to engage all the passengers in a chant before the final stop: "Don't leave anything on the bus!" In short, Winston turned an ordinary bus ride into an extraordinary experience.

As you can imagine, not every conference attendee appreciated Winston's welcoming gestures, jokes, and counsel, preferring silence, especially in the early morning hours. However, because Winston showed a genuine interest in learning about his customers—who they were, where they were from, what they did, why they were in town—he developed a rapport with them that was very unusual. His engaging attitude, authenticity, and ability to connect with others added a dimension to the conference experience that was both memorable and meaningful.

In no uncertain terms, Winston showed that he truly cared about people, that he found meaning in his encounters with his customers, and that he was firmly committed to exploring his personal labyrinth—his inner bus route—through his work as a bus driver. In turn, Winston found deeper meaning in his work, and therefore his work had deeper meaning to him and to those with whom he connected. I pray that Winston survived Katrina and is able to continue his meaning quest, both for his sake and for those people who are fortunate to encounter him.

Working the Corporate Labyrinth

Business leaders and corporate CEOs would be wise to follow Winston's lead, in my opinion. Yet in the corporate world it can be difficult to find the daily moments of connection that nurture meaning. The bottom line is a harsh taskmaster, and the levels of accountability in a business or corporation might not lend themselves to daily gratification. Although the opportunities to honor one another through moments of personal connection may be limited, the need is there. Like everyone else, a business executive needs to feel appreciated, understood, and fulfilled. The opportunities to feel connected beyond the boardroom and office have to be actively sought. And even when successful businesspeople appreciate the link between their inner world and their business bottom line, they find the task is not simply weaving together two ideals but more like creating a complex tapestry, comparable to the design of a labyrinth.

For Tom Chappell, cofounder with his wife Kate of the company Tom's of Maine, coming to terms with his business calling and his spiritual calling is a labyrinth of meaning that has lasted nearly forty years. It has taken him on a personal journey through the most intimate parts of his inner life, even if it did start with clean clothes, safe soil, and toothpaste. Let me explain.

The 1960s and 1970s saw the beginning of the environmental movement. One of the first concerns was the chemical runoff that compromised the health of the soil and ultimately the groundwater systems, oceans, and lakes. In response, Tom Chappell developed Clearlake, a nonphosphate liquid laundry detergent that was environmentally friendly in both product and packaging. Next, Tom's of Maine toothpaste, an all-natural, sugar-free product that did not harm the body, showed up in health-food stores. In those days, customers had to go out of their way to find Tom's of Maine toothpaste — ordinary supermarkets had no natural foods and products sections.

Mostly through word of mouth, Tom's of Maine toothpaste came to symbolize a personal stand on the ecology movement: Why use sugar to clean your teeth if sugar causes cavities? Why hurt the environment if you don't have to? Tom Chappell had taken his personal environmental ethic and applied it directly to his business—in both product and process. Since 1970, Tom's of Maine has flourished. The eco-friendly company has made its living, and its reputation, through its flagship toothpaste brand, as well as mouthwash, flossing ribbon, deodorants, soap, shampoo, shaving cream, decongestants, tonics, and herbal extracts made from natural ingredients and packaged in an environmentally friendly fashion—all now readily available at your local supermarket. Parenthetically, Tom's of Maine was so successful that in 2006 it became part of the Colgate-Palmolive Company, although it still strives to maintain its core values and mission.

Forty years is a long time, however, and naturally Tom Chappell changed. In the mid-1980s, he faced a dilemma that would determine the direction and purpose of his company and of his life. Would Tom's of Maine be a purely profit-based company, or would he base the company's success on what he could achieve with the profits? And there was a yet more compelling existential dilemma: was his company where he really belonged? Tom was feeling called by the Episcopal ministry and was considering leaving the company and going to the seminary.

His labyrinth of meaning required heavy doses of ethical and personal decision making. His business had grown dramatically. The pressure to succeed at the bottom line—above all to grow profits—was reinforced by the MBA mentality of the new professionals who had joined his company. Some of them even wanted him to add saccharin to his toothpaste so it would be more palatable to the mainstream market. His original vision of commitment to natural products was facing compromise by the emphasis on company growth and profits. He no longer felt himself and his values being reflected by the company he had founded, and he found his company less and less fulfilling. He began to search for inspiration elsewhere.

In 1988 he enrolled on a part-time basis at Harvard Divinity School. For the next three years, Chappell spent two and a half days a week in Kennebunk, Maine, running the company, and the remainder of the work week going to school in Cambridge, Massachusetts. At Harvard he studied the writings of the great moral and religious philosophers and tried to relate their ideas to business in general and to Tom's of Maine in particular.

Chappell was influenced by the work of Martin Buber, the twentieth-century Jewish philosopher who argued that we can have either of two opposite attitudes toward others, leading to two very different types of relationships. In the I-It relationship, we treat other people as objects and expect something back from each relationship. In contrast, in the I-Thou relationship we relate to others out of respect, friendship, and love. In other words, we either see others as objects to use for our selfish purposes or we honor people for their own sake. Tom quickly recognized that he and Kate instinctively operated their company using the I-Thou relationship, but his professional managers were following the I-It model.

Chappell was also deeply influenced by the writings of the eighteenth-century American philosopher Jonathan Edwards. Edwards believed that an individual's identity comes not from being separate but from being in relationship with others. Running with this notion, Chappell began thinking of Tom's of Maine in this light, perceiving it not simply as a private company but as a company in direct relationship to employees, customers, suppliers, financial partners, governments, the community, and even the earth itself.

Chappell's vision of his company as a social and moral entity as well as a business organization more deeply reflected his spiritual beliefs, which in turn reinforced his connection to the outside world. His business continues to be a success in the broadest possible terms—satisfying his spiritual yearnings and will to meaning as well as the bottom line. Tom's of Maine, founded on Chappell's youthful ideals, effectively became his mature ministry. Indeed, following the ideals of Viktor Frankl, it can be described as a ministry of meaning.[26]

Finding Our Own Meaning in the Workplace

Meaning can be found anywhere, at any moment. Winston, the bus driver, effectively brings his spiritual self to life by seeing each bus-driving moment and passenger as an opportunity for compassion and connection. Even though his customers pass fleetingly through his life, he finds meaning through the experience of encountering others in his work. Tom Chappell, the unorthodox corporate executive, brings meaning to his multimillion-dollar business through sustained connection to—and creative expression with—his employees, his customers, his products, and the planet.[27]

In the workplace, we can either choose actively to look for and find meaning or we can see our jobs as something outside our "real" lives. If we choose the latter, we cheat ourselves out of an enormous amount of life experience. Even if

Labyrinths of Meaning

we think we hate our jobs, by stopping long enough to connect what we are doing to our broader relationship to meaning, we can find rewards. The question, of course, is do we want to make such a meaningful connection? What if we don't have the personal drive of a Tom Chappell or the human compassion of a Winston? What if we are in mundane jobs that are repetitive and boring?

Our first task is to stop complaining. If we are honest, we know how happy it can make us to find something to complain about in our life, especially at work. It's even more fun if we really do have something, or someone, to complain about. We often seem to create meaning by complaining. This can feel momentarily satisfying, but ultimately it undermines the integrity of our experience. It sucks the meaning out of our work and out of our relationship to our work. This doesn't mean we won't complain once in awhile, perhaps even whine and groan about the job. What it means is that we need to be aware of when and why we are complaining. Is it to bring a moment of simple relief? Or have we started to define our work by negative perceptions?

All of us know people who habitually define their work or job in this negative way, don't we? For example, let's take Bob, who for years has worked in the financial services industry. In fact, Bob has had many moments of apparent career success, having attained key executive positions in several banks, including that of president. Bob's labyrinth of meaning at work, however, has taken him through some dramatic twists and turns, and he rarely, if ever, seems positive or optimistic about his circumstances on the job and, by implication, in his life. As a consequence, Bob complains incessantly about his responsibilities, colleagues, customers, community, and about every other aspect of his working life. If we were to discuss his experiences walking the labyrinth of meaning at work—that is, along his career path—we would hear nothing but stories of misery, negativity, and despair. Unlike Victor Hugo's character Jean Valjean in *Les Misérables*, Bob seems unable (or unwilling) to fulfill his meaning potential, due in large part to his negative, complaining posture toward his work.

Complaining about our miserable jobs around the water-cooler or starting a "bitch and moan club" at the office might offer moments of camaraderie, but it doesn't nurture meaning, for us or for others. The idea that work is neither fun nor fulfilling, nor should it be, takes a huge toll on our ability to bring meaning to our work. When we make complaining a habit, we make meaninglessness a habit. Before long, we are invested in our complaining so deeply that all opportunity to see our work experience as a rich part of our lives vanishes. Instead of taking the time to find meaning, we take the time to find and focus on meaninglessness. So from now on, ask yourself why you complain and, perhaps more important, what's the payoff from your complaining.

Remember also that the great complaint carnival is not a celebration; it's a bandwagon of misery. Our complaints trivialize our experience—both at work and in our personal lives. When we complain, we disconnect. When we complain, we hold whatever or whoever we're complaining about as a shield between us. We perpetuate an old community of victimization and helplessness. But when we take the time to communicate about our fears and insecurities—our real lives—we connect on a deeper, authentic level. When we connect through this deeper humanness, we create a new community of support and possibility—a support that can nurture far beyond the realm of the watercooler.

When we stop long enough to make this kind of authentic connection, we can't avoid meaning. It's waiting for us around every watercooler, in every elevator, every cubbyhole, taxicab, conference room, and corporate boardroom. When we miss the meaning in our work life, we miss the life in our work. And when we miss the life in our work, we can't help but become prisoners of our thoughts—confined within our own inner concentration camp.

Viktor Frankl excavated the darkest despair and discovered meaning. He didn't have to create the meaning—it was there waiting to be found. So it is in our personal and work lives. When we open ourselves to meaning, when we stop long enough to appreciate ourselves and others in meaningful ways, we immediately enhance the quality of our own lives as well as the lives of those around us.

This does not mean that we deny our burdens, our grief, and our worries and sign on to some Pollyannaish perspective of the world. On the contrary. Frankl knew well the meaning of unavoidable suffering through his experience in the Nazi concentration camps. He also knew the darkest human behavior and the brightest light of human possibility—at the same time. He carried the awareness of both potentialities, and this awareness deepened his humanity and created in him a deep and abiding faith. He saw people rise out of the most depraved circumstances and offer all they had to others. He saw the manifestation of spirit on a daily, minute-to-minute basis.

We all know generosity and grace—those moments when

someone says or does just the right thing, offers us the presence we need to see things more clearly, to feel comforted in a difficult time. So why, when so much of our lives happens at work, can't such attention to one another also have a place?

Our lives present us with a labyrinth of meaning, and so do our jobs, our careers, our livelihoods, our "work." And the meaning is not always evident. Life and relationships unfold; they change; we change; sometimes we embrace the process; sometimes we change our circumstances and start over. This is true in work as well as in our private lives. Again, it is part of the labyrinth of our life. We are on one path and it takes us through many turns of fate and fortune, pain and pleasure, loss and gain. It is a path that shapes us, that uncovers our fears, that tests our courage, and that leads us to this very moment. It is a sacred path of individuality, and no one walks it but us.

It is not easy to stay the course with reverence while walking the labyrinth. But no matter what our faith persuasion is—or whether we even have one—honoring our own path is essential if we are to know authentic meaning in our lives. And only when we know meaning in our lives can we really know meaning in our work. *Our will to meaning, not our will to pleasure or our will to power, is what illuminates our lives with true freedom.* This is an extremely important distinction to make as we explore the ways in which we bring our will to bear on our lives and in our work. In the final analysis, we are free to choose our responses to everything that happens in our lives, including those things that happen through our work. This strikes at the very heart of Frankl's teachings and is the basis of the core principle to be explored in the next chapter.

Labyrinths of Meaning

Meaning Moment Recall a situation in your personal life or work life in which you were faced with a major decision to shift direction (this may even be your situation today). Perhaps you were faced with a family member or friend who was challenging your lifestyle habits or way of interacting with others. Perhaps you were faced with a boss or co-worker who was challenging your style or method of doing your job or fulfilling your responsibilities. Or maybe you found yourself in some kind of ethical dilemma or value conflict that pressured you to change direction in some way, whether in your personal life or at work. What, if anything, did you actually do about it? As you think about the situation now, what did you learn from it? What could you have done differently?

 Meaning Question: How do you deal with negativity and habitual complaining in the workplace? In your personal life?

FOR FURTHER REFLECTION

How might the labyrinth metaphor help you find greater meaning and fulfillment in your personal life and work? Think about how you might use this metaphor in a constructive way with your co-workers and with your family members and friends.

Exercise the Freedom
to Choose Your Attitude

*Everything can be taken from a man but . . .
the last of the human freedoms — to choose one's attitude
in any given set of circumstances, to choose one's way.*[28]

It was nearly midnight. It was time to jot down his final
thoughts before darkness fell around him. In just a few minutes, the lights would go out and his cell would no longer be
a "writer's study"; it would be a stark, confining dungeon. For
almost twenty years, this had been his home, his office, and
his prison. But even though he knew it was not likely that he
would ever see real freedom again, he remained true to his
core values and life goals. He wrote several book-length manuscripts, stayed in touch with his loved ones, and persevered
with optimism. His defiant human spirit prevailed.

With a great deal of pride, I can tell you that he is my
great-uncle, General Stylianos Pattakos, a Greek patriot who
served his country as a military officer and political leader
through some of the most turbulent times in modern Greek
history. Among other things, my uncle Stelios was one of

three officers responsible for setting up a military regime in Greece in 1967. He served in various ways, including as the country's vice president, until another government takeover in 1974.

Because of his role in the so-called Greek junta, Uncle Stelios was charged with the crime of treason and imprisoned. Thankfully, there was enough support for him as a person and as a Greek patriot that eventually his role in history was reconsidered and his life spared. In 1995, he was released and was finally able to share his story. As of this writing, Uncle Stelios, who is ninety-eight years old and in good health, has written ten books that comprise his personal memoir and an account of Greek political events.

Like the renowned Viktor Frankl, Nelson Mandela, U.S. Senator John McCain, and Burma's Aung San Suu Kyi—along with numerous unknown courageous and imprisoned people—Uncle Stelios was challenged to understand the deeper meaning of freedom as he dealt with the loss of personal liberties and human dignity. In other words, despite his physical incarceration, my uncle Stelios was called upon to rely on his will to meaning to gain a different kind of freedom—one from within himself—so that he could survive his long ordeal in prison. Putting political views aside, I want to emphasize the primary role that the will to meaning plays as an *intrinsic* motivation for surviving extremely harsh circumstances such as imprisonment and other forms of inescapable human suffering.

A story about Nelson Mandela, former president of South Africa and winner of the Nobel Peace Prize, illuminates the relationship between personal freedom and imprisonment. The day that Mandela was released from prison on Robben Island, Bill Clinton, then governor of Arkansas, was watching the news. He quickly called his wife and daughter and said, "You must see this, it is historic." As Mandela stepped out, Clinton saw a flush of anger on his face as he looked at the people watching; then it disappeared.

Later, when Clinton was president of the United States and Mandela was president of South Africa, the two leaders met, and Clinton relayed his observation during Mandela's release from prison. And because Mandela had always been a model of reconciliation with no spirit of revenge or negativism, President Clinton candidly asked him to explain what seemed to have occurred on that day. President Mandela replied, "Yes, you are right. When I was in prison, the son of a guard started a Bible study and I attended; . . . and that day when I stepped out of prison and looked at the people observing, a flush of anger hit me with the thought that they had robbed me of twenty-seven years. Then the Spirit of Jesus said to me, 'Nelson, while you were in prison you were free; now that you are free, don't become their prisoner.'"[29]

It's neither proper nor possible to compare the ways in which each of these people endured unthinkable experiences. But in their presence in our lives, they represent all people who experienced suffering and triumphed, each in his or her own way. These people were compelled, under uniquely dreadful circumstances, to find meaning within their imprisoned lives. Stripped of most of the freedoms we take for granted, as prisoners they were left with what Frankl called the "last of the human freedoms"—the freedom to choose their attitude in response to their life circumstances.

The Real Superman

This freedom to choose is available in every aspect of our lives. Yet it can be difficult, even when our lives are comparably safe and perceivably free, to do so. We all struggle with situations beyond our control. Bringing these aspects of our lives under our control—even if it is only our attitude toward the situations—is where our freedom takes shape, no matter what the circumstances.

Christopher Reeve had it all. In addition to his early success on Broadway, he was known all over the world for his leading role in *Superman*, the movie that made him a star. At the age of forty-two, his acting career was bright and his life was filled with unlimited possibilities. He was passionate about life on all levels and was intent on experiencing it with gusto. An all-around athlete, Reeve loved sailing and was a skilled equestrian, skier, ice skater, and tennis player.

On Memorial Day 1995, however, the world held its breath as Christopher Reeve struggled for life. Reeve had been thrown from his horse in an accident that broke his neck and left him unable to move or breathe. The man who was Superman had become quadriplegic. But, as he wrote in his best-selling autobiography, appropriately entitled *Still Me*, "I think a hero is an ordinary individual who finds strength to persevere and endure in spite of overwhelming obstacles."[30] And so the story of the real Superman continued.

In the years after the accident, Reeve not only survived but thrived—fighting for himself, for his family, and for thousands of people with spinal cord injuries in the United States and around the world. An inspirational force, Reeve displayed his choice to maintain a positive attitude toward his situation on *Larry King Live*, just ten months after his accident: "I am a very lucky guy," he said. "I can testify before Congress. I can raise funds. I can raise awareness."[31]

Christopher Reeve credited his wife, Dana, and his three children for quickly lifting him out of an initial morass of hopelessness. "You learn the stuff of your life (sports, movies)...that's not the essence of your existence," he said. "My relationships were always good. Now they have transcended. That's why I can honestly say I am a lucky man." He goes further:

> When a catastrophe happens, it's easy to feel so sorry for yourself that you can't see anybody around you. But the way out is through your **relationships** [emphasis added]. The way out of that misery or obsession is to focus more on what your little boy needs or what your teenagers need or what other people around you need. It's very hard to do, and often you have to force yourself. But that is the answer to the dilemma of being frozen—at least it's the answer I found.[32]

Again we see it was the fact that Christopher Reeve exercised his freedom to choose his attitude about his life and work that enabled him to take the bold steps of confronting the unforeseen changes in his life path. By doing so, he was able to do more than simply cope with his personal suffering and loss. Reeve also unleashed his potential for self-healing and discovered a path to authentic meaning that might have gone unnoticed. As a by-product of his conscious choice, he was able to remind us that life is not to be taken for granted but to be lived fully, with passion, curiosity, and gratitude.[33]

Reeve was also an inspirational role model for others. Most notably, his positive attitude directly influenced his wife,

Dana, who not only took care of him for almost ten years after his riding accident but who also experienced another personal tragedy. In August 2005, even though she had never smoked in her life, Dana was diagnosed with lung cancer. The announcement came less than a year after Christopher's passing. Yet I vividly remember watching Dana on television, still in an upbeat mood. When she was asked how she maintained such a positive outlook on life, Dana replied that she had had a "good teacher"—her husband. The American actress, singer, activist for disability causes, and wife of the real Superman died on March 6, 2006, at the age of forty-four.

In life's most difficult situations, our capacity to cope and our personal resilience are put to the test. It is then that the freedom to choose our attitude takes center stage. To exercise this freedom effectively, we must be able to view our situation from different vantage points; know who we are; and be flexible and courageous enough to change when necessary, even if it means moving away from what is expected or considered normal.

The responsibility for choosing our attitude lies solely with each of us. It cannot be transferred to someone else. This ultimate responsibility applies both to our personal and to our work lives. I have made this claim over the years to various corporate and government clients, especially in cases where workers, including executives and managers, seem intent on complaining about their working conditions rather than doing anything to change the situation. I'm reminded of a *Far Side* cartoon that shows people mingling at a "Part of the Problem" Convention—it illustrates to an absurd level how limited and negative our thinking can become. We celebrate our freedom to choose our attitude at work only when we decide to move from being a part of the problem to becoming a part of the solution.

In our personal lives, too, it doesn't work to wait for solutions magically to arrive; we have to be a part of the solution. NBA coach Phil Jackson, in his book *Sacred Hoops*, cautions us to remember that the best way to realize your dreams is to wake up! In other words, being part of any solution means taking action. And taking action involves more than just dreaming, no matter how vivid, how real, your dreams appear to be.

Learning to Cope

Through our life experiences and the investment we make in personal growth and development, our repertoire of coping skills can and usually does change over time. We invest in ourselves—through such things as training or counseling—and the return on this investment is increased effectiveness in dealing with life's situations: we build our capacity for accommodating change and managing transitions, even those that may appear to be out of our control, and we grow more resilient to the ebb and flow of life.

In Frankl's case, had he not adopted his coping beliefs upon his arrival at Auschwitz, he might not have been able to sustain his optimistic and passionate view about his chances of survival:

> *Unless there was a 100% guarantee that I will be killed here on the spot, and I will never survive this concentration camp last part of my life, unless there is any guarantee, I'm responsible for living from now on in a way that I may make use of the slightest chance of survival, ignoring the great danger surrounding me in also all*

the following camps I had been sent. This, as it were, a coping, not mechanism, but a coping maxim I adopted, I espoused, at that moment.[34]

By choosing his fundamental attitude, which he called his "coping maxim," the coping mechanisms in his psychiatrist toolkit became more meaningful and effective. His decision to experience meaning under desperate circumstances enabled him to act on his own behalf as well as on behalf of others.

What lessons can we learn from Frankl's experience? Think about difficult situations in your personal life or work in which your attitude played a defining role in how well you were able to cope. Think about the coping mechanisms that were at your disposal. Did you choose to use them? Why or why not? How effective were you in coping with the situation? Now ask yourself a more fundamental question: What guides your coping skills? What principle or principles underlie your decision making in complex, challenging situations? It can be difficult to articulate these deeper ideals and values in our lives. If nothing definitive comes immediately to mind, jot down your initial thoughts on this question for later use in framing a more complete answer.

Ponder also the times when you observed people who were guided by their coping skills in difficult decision-making situations. You can probably identify cases of extraordinary resolve by your co-workers, family members, or friends during times of hardship—personal or professional. Although these situations may not have been as catastrophic as that experienced by Viktor Frankl, they may still have been formidable challenges to overcome or survive.

In the workplace, it is clear that some individuals are able to cope more easily than others with the outpouring of professional and occupational changes in today's job market. Corporate downsizing, mergers and acquisitions, new technologies, career or job shifts, new working arrangements, and the trauma of unemployment are all part of our work lives. All of us can tell stories that illustrate the many ways in which people respond to these challenges. In the final analysis, the most capable, responsible, and resilient individuals have adopted, consciously or unconsciously, a coping maxim and skills to guide and drive them toward meaningful resolutions.

When we choose our attitude in light of what I would call true optimism, we actually make three choices:

1. We choose a positive attitude about the situation at hand.

2. We choose an attitude that supports a form of creative visualization about what's possible.

3. We choose an attitude that generates passion for the action that makes the possible become a reality.

In other words, being a true optimist requires more than positive thinking. Positive affirmations, like good intentions, aren't enough; we need to be able to visualize the possibilities that may result from our choice of attitude, and be able to feel the passion behind our choice of attitude that will help us actualize those possibilities. We each have the freedom to make these choices, but it is amazing how frequently we don't. We either choose to abstain from taking full responsibility for what should be our conscious choices or choose, albeit unconsciously, to remain frozen in thought patterns that may no longer serve our highest good. In short, we become prisoners of our thoughts.

In my life and work, I have encountered clients, co-workers, friends, and family members who are stuck in old habits of self-imprisonment. They display the power of negative thinking about a work or life situation, ensuring that they could never visualize a better tomorrow. Or they are so fearful of the unknown that they have essentially immobilized themselves, effectively avoiding any kind of risk. The ultimate freedom to choose their attitude and their future, no matter how desperate they may be, seems as foreign to them as a life in which they could feel fulfilled and happy.

I have seen many workplace situations in which organizational change has resulted in people losing their jobs. In one case, I had a friend, Tom, who had been let go by a high-tech firm after many years of faithful service. Although Tom clearly did not agree with the company's decision to release him, and he felt that his value was neither acknowledged nor fully understood, he realized that he was given no choice but to move on with his life.

Ironically, Tom had discussed leaving the company many times in the past, but he couldn't bring himself to make the decision to leave on his own. And although he felt positive about his chances for a new position or new work, he was unable to visualize the possibilities. He even shared with me that he could not see himself doing something else. When the company's decision to release him finally became a reality, he was forced to change his attitude.

"For the most part," he said, "my mind is racing a thousand miles an hour—which in itself is absolutely great. Maybe uncertainty brings out the best in us."

Forced to take a leap, Tom changed his attitude about his freedom and was thus able to change his attitude about his future. He is now combining several opportunities that more accurately reflect his deep passion, values, and interests. Ironically, it took the company's decision to let him go before he was able to see the possibility of realizing his meaning potential, his will to meaning.

To show that it is never too late, let me share another example of how the freedom to choose your attitude can be exercised in a work-related situation. One of my good friends and colleagues was a creativity consultant in her late eighties. Like Viktor Frankl, Rebecca was a source of insight and inspiration, especially for those a lot younger who are facing changing circumstances. Because of a severe hip injury, Rebecca was confined to a wheelchair, which severely restricted her ability to move around, travel, and generally live her active life. Refusing to be dismayed, she remained positive about her plight, visualized a redesigned work situation for herself, and took action to bring it about—all at the age of eighty-nine years young! Rebecca continued to consult with individuals and organizations, but with a renewed focus on disabled workers, until her passing several years later. More than simply positive thinking, hers was a case of true optimism. She exercised her freedom to choose her attitude under difficult circumstances and expanded her life creatively in a new way.

Here's another person who demonstrates the ageless wisdom of true optimism. In October 2006, Ralph Waldo McBurney, usually known as Waldo, was recognized as the oldest worker in America by Experience Works. At the time he was 104 years old and was recognized as a national symbol for his longevity and work ethic. An avid runner, Waldo set international records in track and field events and was still competing well after his 101st birthday! One of the most remarkable things about Waldo and his life story, however, is that he published his first book in 2004. I proudly display Waldo's book in my personal library for what it says about life and for its inspirational title: *My First 100 Years!* How's that for choosing a positive attitude and being a true optimist? Although Waldo left us in July 2009, when he was almost 107 years old, his life-affirming legacy will live forever.

Exercising Your Freedom

We all have this ultimate freedom to choose our attitude, but each of us must make an active choice to exercise our freedom. Often we are unaware of our attitudes toward something (or someone), or we may not want to address the possibility of changing our attitude—let alone be willing to do so. So when you face a challenging situation, these are the first questions to ask yourself: Am I aware of my current attitude toward the situation? If necessary, am I willing to change my attitude?

This reminds me of a conversation that I had with one reader of *Prisoners of Our Thoughts*, a physician. He said, "Alex, I really like your book. I only have one question. I don't really understand the first principle: Exercise the freedom to choose your attitude. Why would I want to do that if I already have an attitude?"

Obviously, this particular reader didn't get the message I was trying to convey! Fortunately, after some discussion, he understood the meaning behind the principle and has used it effectively in his medical practice (for example, as a way to improve doctor-patient communication) and his personal life ever since.

Here is a quick exercise that can help you address these questions and issues, not only by opening up new possibilities but also by helping you to exercise your freedom to choose your attitude.

To begin, think of a situation in your personal life or at work that is or was especially stressful, negative, or challenging for you. Now take a deep breath, and write down ten positive things that could result—or did result—from this situation. Notice any resistance you have to doing this. (Sometimes it's easier to stay mad, self-righteous, or right.) But just let your mind loose and entertain the possibilities. Write down whatever comes to mind first. Continue to stretch your imagination and suspend judgment, listing whatever comes into consciousness, no matter how silly, far out, or unrealistic your thoughts appear to be. Feel completely free to determine or define what positive means to you.

After you have completed your list, look at it closely and let the positive become possible in your thinking about the difficult situation. Sometimes this is very hard to do. It requires letting go of old ways of thinking, of pain, remorse, disappointment, frustration, perhaps even of grief and anguish. But this exercise levels your playing field of possibilities for the future and opens you to deep optimism no matter how challenging your circumstances.

When I was introduced to this exercise, I was given the following instruction: "List ten positive things if you died today." I was unaccustomed to discussing, let alone exploring, the possibilities of my death and thought the exercise totally absurd. It turned out to be the opposite. In fact, the participants at my session, including yours truly, had a great deal of fun with this exercise once we allowed ourselves the freedom to let go. Most of us were eventually able to see the silver lining in something even as catastrophic as our death. Our group energy increased dramatically, and we all had opportunities to learn new things about ourselves, each other, and the often-taboo topic of death. I have since used this exercise with hundreds of client groups with similar success.

If we can find something positive to say about our own death, it should be easy to find something positive to say about our work situation, family life, and so forth, don't you think? My experience over many years is that no matter how catastrophic the event seems, whether personal or work-related, eventually something positive *always* results from it.

Let me share a personal experience that may help to clarify what I mean. Years ago, while still a full-time professor, I was driving to campus early one morning to teach a class. It was a very peaceful morning, there was no traffic, and I was enjoying the solitude as I listened to relaxing music on the radio. I remember driving down a tree-lined street, with a grass island in the center and cars parked tightly on both sides. Coming up the street toward me was a school bus van, the only other moving vehicle in sight. Suddenly, for no apparent reason, I saw the van veer out of control and crash into one of the parked cars on its side of the street. I couldn't believe it! Immediately I stopped my car and rushed over to the van to see what I could do.

The front of the van was crushed, and I could see and smell smoke. While I prayed that someone in the neighborhood had heard the crash and called 911, I pulled the driver, a young woman, out of the vehicle and, as carefully as I could, carried her to a nearby lawn. I could tell she was injured and upset by what had happened. She began to cry as she wailed, "Oh, no, what am I going to do? I just got this job; my parents are going to kill me!"

Still waiting for someone, preferably an ambulance, to arrive and help with the situation, I was at a loss for what to do at that particular moment. I wanted to keep the young woman as calm as possible. Without really thinking about the consequences, I looked her straight in the eyes and said: "Let's list ten positive things about this accident." I started with: (1) there were no children in the school van; (2) there was nobody in the parked car that was struck; (3) neither vehicle had exploded or was on fire, at least not at that point; (4) somebody was around to help her in her moment of need; and (5) she's still alive and conscious. By the time we identified only a few of the items on the list of positives, the driver actually began to smile! When the ambulance finally arrived, and I explained to the emergency medical technician what we had done while waiting, he said that her shift in attitude had most likely prevented her from going into shock.

A key lesson to be learned from this experience: even if you don't see the cognitive or emotional benefits of maintaining a positive attitude toward a situation you are facing, whether it is at work or in your personal life, please consider the physiological benefits. One of the real powers of positive thinking is that it is good for your health!

From the perspective of work, here now are some trigger questions that have been posed in a number of settings:

- List ten positive things that would happen if you lost your job today.

- List ten positive things that would happen if your department was eliminated.

- List ten positive things that would happen from a breakdown in a production line.

- List ten positive things that would happen if the work week was changed from five days/eight hours per day to four days/ten hours per day.

- List ten positive things that would happen from a 20 percent budget cut.

In each of these situations benefits were found, both in process and product outcomes. First, everyone involved acknowledged that they were free to choose their attitude and view their situation from many different perspectives. Second, no matter how desperate the situation or condition confronted, everyone acknowledged that something positive could result, even in the situations that seemed ridiculous at first. Also, in responding to these questions, the positive energy among individuals, especially in work groups or teams, increased dramatically. The varied opportunities to view the situation or condition in a new light increased, as did the ideas and opportunities to resolve the challenges. Through this exercise, the participants learned an effective way to release themselves at least partly from their self-imposed thought prisons.

Before moving on, let me share a few more practical illustrations of how this exercise can work in everyday life and at work. Let's start with a unique application of the Ten Positive Things Exercise in the workplace. The situation involved a client training session I was conducting in Alaska with the U.S. Forest Service. At the end of the first day of a two-day session, I overheard comments from one of the more macho male participants, Paul, that he was not at all interested in the training and didn't feel that it was relevant to him. The Ten Positive Things Exercise had been introduced and practiced that afternoon, and Paul obviously was not impressed.

The next morning when I returned to the training venue, I noticed Paul sitting beside two female participants, laughing and giggling. When I asked him what had happened, he reported that when he went home the evening after our session, he was shocked to learn that his teenage daughter had received a tongue piercing and was now sporting a new piece of jewelry in her mouth. Angry and upset, Paul argued with his daughter and wife; in short, he had a terrible night with his family. When he returned to the training session, looking tired and depressed, he confessed to his two female co-workers what had happened. Immediately, they asked him to list ten positive things from his daughter's tongue piercing. Working together, they not only came up with many potential positives to be gained from his stressful experience (for example, his daughter wasn't pregnant, she hadn't gotten a tattoo) but also fostered an entirely new—and positive—attitude toward his daughter and the training session! Indeed, things could have been worse for his teenage daughter, and doing the exercise put this situation in perspective for Paul and helped him change his attitude about it.

Here's another example of this exercise in action—with a unique twist. It proved to be a rather strange yet deeply meaningful experience. I had been asked to conduct a workshop on the principles in *Prisoners of Our Thoughts* for inmates at a state penitentiary. The idea of discussing ways to escape one's inner mental prison with actual inmates, many of whom had served or had been sentenced to serve many years in prison, was an unusual and challenging opportunity for me. Indeed, this invitation forced me to practice what I preach in one of the most humbling and learning-intensive environments I had ever encountered. Like the Asian Tsunami disaster relief experience described in the preface, this situation posed an extraordinary acid test of the meaning-centered principles in action.

"Okay, everyone, I now would like you to list ten positive things about being in prison," I told the group of about two dozen inmates, who looked at me like I was crazy. In a room designated primarily for education and training purposes, the inmates sat at tables arranged in a circle and began writing (each participant had been given a pad of paper and a small pencil, which were confiscated immediately at the end of the session for security). Some inmates grumbled and some laughed at what they had been asked to do, but all participated in the exercise in one way or another.

As expected, some participants were unable to find anything positive in their incarceration, at least until they heard what their fellow inmates had to say. Some participants were very serious in the way they framed their responses to this exercise, while others let their imaginations soar with a sense of humor that might have seemed out of place under such circumstances.

Here are some examples across the spectrum of what was said:

- "Society is now protected from me since I'm locked up."
- "I now know what I don't want to do with (the rest of) my life."
- "I can be a role model for others so that they don't do what I did."
- "I'm no longer homeless!"
- "I've learned who my real friends are and who aren't."
- "I've been reborn and now value life and freedom like never before."
- "I get to work out a lot."

Of course these reflections comprise only a quick snapshot of what was shared by the participants. The exercise was able to lift the heavy weight of the energy in the room and tap into the human spirit of all participants. They no longer had to think and act only as prison inmates, so each person could experience, even with a sense of humor, the sharing of his authentic thoughts and feelings with the others. In turn, the experience enabled everyone to explore what some might call the silver lining in their personalized life predicaments. And by being challenged *not* to be prisoners of their thoughts, even though they were obviously prisoners by definition, all participants had the chance to exercise the freedom to choose their attitude—the ultimate freedom of all human beings—in spite of the circumstance of being physically incarcerated in an actual prison from which they could not escape!

Finally, here is a situation that involved another reader of *Prisoners of Our Thoughts* who was having difficulty grasping and applying the notion that he had the freedom to choose his attitude even under trying circumstances. Mark had just learned that his wife of twenty-four years had been diagnosed with breast cancer. It was an aggressive cancer, found in two spots, one of which was invasive. Mark was devastated and told me that he first experienced shock and disbelief, along with a heavy dose of denial, followed by what he described as "God-awful anxiety." For several days after learning about his wife's disease, "the longest of my life," Mark couldn't stop crying. In short, he didn't know what to do.

In the midst of his despair, Mark remembered the Ten Positive Things Exercise he had read about in my book and decided with his wife to give it a shot. Here are some of the items on their list of positives that they shared with me:

1. My wife went by herself for the biopsy results. At first, I was angry as I felt it was my place to accompany her. Then I had the realization that for her, it was an act of bravery to spare me. She called one of my friends at work and asked him to come to my office so that I wouldn't be alone when she phoned me with the bad news. I'm privileged to have a marriage where a spouse can demonstrate that depth of caring for me.

2. Two years ago I (Mark) went through a challenging double hip replacement. The immediate surgery, rehabilitation, pain tolerance, etc., took about twelve weeks. One achieves a sense of almost total normalcy in about a year. During this time I took the opportunity to lose weight, improve my health, and get as fit as I've ever been in my life. Somehow, in some way, I'm wondering if all of this took place first as preparation for the battle to come. If I ever needed to be physically ready, now is the time.

3. Family, neighbors, and friends have drawn together as a tribe now united in a sacred battle to save my wife's life. I've witnessed so many people demonstrate their support and caring that I'm left somewhat speechless. My wife is fiercely loved by many, many people and I, too, am the recipient of their support.

4. It's almost as if my whole life has been a preparation for this test. In some uncanny way I feel like this is exactly where I belong. Make no mistake, I'm terrified. But I'm also resolved to stand my ground with her come what may.

5. I tend to be a skeptic and somewhat pessimistic by nature. Right now, my wife is asking me to help her attach to her anger. She wants to fight and she wants me to get her mad enough to survive. I am now being given the supreme opportunity to relentlessly practice being positive, day in and day out. Minute by minute. If ever I had a moment of swallowing my fear and acting in spite of it, this was it.

6. She and I have confirmed how close we are, but our intimacy is only going to increase in the days ahead. Love is a profoundly mysterious thing.

7. As humans, we tend to see a lifespan as having a narrative arc—from childhood to old age. Any interruption of the unfolding story is seen as tragic. Maybe that's not it at all. Maybe the universe exists because goodness requires it. And maybe what it's all about is that humans were to evolve to discover/create love and meaning—because that's God's nature expressing itself. If that's at least possible, then my wife has accomplished many lifetimes already through her children, her friends, and her relationship with me. That can never be undone; it exists forever.

I thank Mark (not his real name) and his wife for sharing their very personal experience with me. Again, as Frankl advised, the way that people accept their fate — those things beyond their control — can add deeper meaning to their life. Such has proven to be the case for Mark and his wife. Through their inescapable suffering, their lives have been enriched with new-found meaning. As they continue to wage their battle with the disease and seek a path to recovery, this meaning will always be with them, providing much-needed support and strength along the way.

> As a human phenomenon, however, freedom is all too human. Human freedom is finite freedom. Man is not free from conditions. But he is free to take a stand in regard to them. The conditions do not completely condition him. Within limits it is up to him whether or not he succumbs and surrenders to the conditions. He may as well rise above them and by so doing open up and enter the human dimension. . . . Ultimately, man is not subject to the conditions that confront him; rather, these conditions are subject to his decision. Wittingly or unwittingly, he decides whether he will face up or give in, whether or not he will let himself be determined by the conditions.[35]

We have courageous role models to learn from as we explore the vast reaches of our own freedom. Many are public heroes, honored by history or celebrity status. Others can be found in our friends, in our families, and in our communities. My own Uncle Stelios, through his choices, attitudes, and commitment to his own values and future, embodies for me the many facets of Viktor Frankl's meaning-centered philosophy. Although we may not be totally free from the conditions or situations that confront us — in our personal and work lives — the important thing is that we can choose how we respond, at least through our choice of attitude. According to Frankl, this is not only our right as human beings; it is our full human beingness to be free. All we have to do is resist the temptation of remaining a prisoner of our thoughts and choose this freedom, no matter what.

 Recall a situation in your personal or work life in which you consciously exercised the freedom to choose your attitude about it (this may even be your situation today). Perhaps you were faced with a difficult relationship with a family member or friend or were facing a difficult boss or co-worker. Or perhaps you were confronted by a change in living arrangements, health status, or job/career. What was your attitude at first toward the situation? How did your attitude change? What, if anything, did you actually do about changing your attitude? As you think about the situation now, what did you learn from it? What could you have done differently?

 Meaning Question: How do you maintain a positive attitude in your personal life and at work?

FOR FURTHER REFLECTION

How might Frankl's notion of a coping maxim (an overall belief about coping) help you find greater meaning and fulfillment in your personal life and work? Think also about how you might use this technique in a positive, constructive way with your family, friends, and others in your personal life, as well as at work with your colleagues.

Exercise the Freedom to Choose Your Attitude

Realize Your Will
to Meaning

A man who becomes conscious of the responsibility he bears toward
a human being who affectionately waits for him, or to an unfinished
work, will never be able to throw away his life. He knows the "why" for
his existence, and will be able to bear almost any "how."[36]

"It's going to be a fun week, sailing the *Endeavor*, tennis, golf, eating, drinking. All the things we are best known for," said former Tyco CEO Dennis Kozlowski. This statement was recorded on a videotape of a two-million-dollar birthday bash that Kozlowski threw for his wife on the island of Sardinia in 2000. An edited version of the tape was shown to jurors at Kozlowski's larceny trial, providing further evidence that Tyco had funded its ex-CEO's lavish lifestyle for years before he resigned in June 2002. Alas, Sigmund Freud would be proud, for Dennis Kozlowski demonstrated that Freud's theory of the pleasure principle, also known as the will to pleasure, is alive and well in corporate America!

Tyco, of course, is not the only major company in recent times that has faced public scrutiny and the wrath of government regulators and the courts because of corporate scandals.

Nor is Kozlowski the only corporate executive to have gained such infamous notoriety. Do the names Ken Lay (Enron), Bernie Ebbers (Worldcom), and Martha Stewart ring a bell? And what about Bernard Madoff, the former chairman of the NASDAQ Stock Exchange and Ponzi scheme master—to say nothing of the illicit dealings of those CEOs and other executives, on and off Wall Street, associated with government bailouts of firms that were deemed too big to fail during the financial meltdown and economic crisis of 2008 and after? Incidentally, there are Web sites dedicated to profiling many of these individuals and highlighting the most notorious of the corporate scandals in which they were involved.[37] Unlike Tyco's Kozlowski, it should be noted that many of these executives did (or do) not appear as interested in following Freud's will to pleasure as they were (or are) in pursuing Alfred Adler's will to power (in Adler's words, "striving for superiority"). Adler, you may remember, was a contemporary and mentor of Viktor Frankl.

To Frankl, however, both Freud's will to pleasure and Adler's will to power were manifestations of something missing, which hinted that there was another explanation for the kinds of behaviors exhibited by the former corporate icons identified here. In effect, the need or drive to seek pleasure à la Freud and the relentless pursuit of power à la Adler were really just attempts to cover up—but not necessarily fill—a void of meaning in the lives of these individuals. Put differently, because their will to meaning had been frustrated, for whatever reasons, they chose alternative paths to follow—paths based on the premise that pleasure or power or both would be able to replace what had been missing.

Only the search for meaning, Frankl would say, holds the potential to bring the kind of authentic enrichment and fulfillment that most people desire from their work and in their personal lives. And it is the ability to realize our will to meaning—our authentic commitment to meaningful values and goals that only we can actualize and fulfill—that guides us in the quest to tap into this distinctly human potential. Unlike Freud or Adler, Frankl considers this the main concern of human beings, rather than the gratification of drives and instincts.

We've seen examples of people, including corporate executives, who demonstrate the central importance of Frankl's will to meaning in their work lives (for example, Tom Chappell of Tom's of Maine). While such individuals may also want (or seek) pleasure and authority, that is not their primary motivation. Other examples are Bill Hewlett and David Packard, who built their company, Hewlett-Packard, from its start in a one-car garage into one of the world's most admired success stories, guided by a particular set of meaningful values, known as the HP Way, for identifying and meeting their objectives, working with one another, and dealing with customers, shareholders, and others.[38]

It is important to recognize that not all values are created equal. Actualizing such values as those associated exclusively with pleasure and power would not, for Frankl, constitute the way to fulfill authentic meaning. Instead we might consider something said to me by a government employee, who referred to values as the "things that make life worth living." In other words, by relying on our moral compass, or what psychologist and author James Hillman refers to as our "soul's code,"[39] we may uncover values that are deeply meaningful and worth pursuing in our work and in our personal lives. As we shall see in this chapter, a personal (and organizational) commitment to such positive, life-affirming values is clearly a manifestation of Frankl's will to meaning!

Searching for Pleasure and Power

How many of us have looked forward to a beautifully planned holiday and then felt disappointed after it was over? How often does the promise of pleasure captivate us, only to leave us unsatisfied afterward, no matter how perfect it seemed at the time? This is true with everything from drugs and sex to pay raises and vacations. It's the *promise*, the anticipation of pleasure that we are lured by; pleasure itself is fleeting and often hard to capture. We come down with a cold on the plane to paradise. We receive a sad phone call from a family member that dashes plans for a romantic evening. Our teenage daughter or son puts a dent in the new car and it's no longer perfect. We feel excited about what we purchased during a shopping spree, only to find the thrill gone after a week. Moments of true pleasure—like authentic happiness—come to us when we aren't looking for them. They are unexpected gifts, moments that transcend our planning and even our perception of pleasure.

The search for power in our lives is parallel to our search for pleasure. It too is "out there." Power over our employees, our bosses, our customers, our shareholders, our kids, the waitress in a restaurant, or a clerk in a retail store is illusory at best and terribly destructive at worst. We think we might have power, but we never know for sure. Even if we do, in the power game there's always an opponent; the ground is always shifting. Much like Sisyphus, the Greek hero who was ordered by the gods to push a big rock uphill only to see it slip out of his hands at the last moment, our search for power becomes an endless—and joyless—undertaking.

A few decades ago, when group therapy took center stage in the self-awareness movement, one exercise in particular illuminated the power principle. A group was asked to spend some time together to choose a leader. After they had carefully selected a leader, the group was then asked to go back and select the person most responsible for choosing the leader. It was the leader behind the leader who was the real leader. When power is the stage, there's always another power waiting in the wings. Power is an exhausting game to play and, like pleasure, power is fleeting and always subject to unforeseen forces.

Yet these two principles in life—power and pleasure—have been the focus of much attention and analysis in psychotherapy and have been used as platforms for designing and managing organizations and work. As we have already discussed, the father of psychoanalysis, Sigmund Freud, weighed in on the pleasure principle; Alfred Adler, also known as the founder of individual psychology, weighed in on the will to power. A huge body of work has gone into defining us by these principles—both of which involve forces from outside ourselves.

Here, in the vast exploration of our inner and outer lives, Frankl's will to meaning rises above and distinguishes itself from the will to pleasure and the will to power. The will to meaning comes from *within*. Only we can find it, control it, and fulfill it. It is meaning that sustains us throughout our lives, no matter how little or how much power and pleasure come our way. Most important of all, meaning sustains us through any pain and suffering we must endure.

In his book *Full Catastrophe Living*, Jon Kabat-Zinn writes about staying connected to our original wholeness no matter what challenges to our health, well-being, and welfare we face. His book explores the lives of many people for whom life-threatening illness became a transforming experience. They connected not only to others in a way that anchored them in love, acceptance, and forgiveness, but also to themselves. Some survived and triumphed over illness, while others didn't. However, they all deepened their experience in ways that honored meaning in their lives as well as in death.

When we take the time to cultivate our relationship to our original self, all our experience becomes grounded in meaning. This was true for Frankl when he observed the behavior of those imprisoned in the Nazi concentration camps; it was true for those interviewed throughout Kabat-Zinn's book; and it's true for anyone who has survived tragedy and allowed their grief to break open their heart to tenderness. When tenderness prevails, we love and forgive ourselves and others. When the opposite happens, when bitterness seals our hearts shut, we are isolated from ourselves, from others, and ultimately from meaning itself.

If we take the time to think about our friends, we all know someone who has survived tragedy yet somehow retained deep cheerfulness and optimism as the way through life. One person I know, Charlotte, not long ago lost a twenty-one-year-old son who had suffered from autism. Only months before her son's death, I spoke with Charlotte about the challenges and, yes, burden of raising an autistic child. Charlotte described the experience candidly, noting that it was not always easy for her or her husband over so many years. She recalled reading Frankl's book *Man's Search for Meaning* on several occasions during this time, underscoring its influence on her thinking and actions during some of the most difficult moments. Charlotte was able to find deeper meaning in her experience as a parent, no matter how difficult the challenges were, and she learned much about her own humanness through her relationship with her disabled son. When her son died suddenly at such an early age, it became clear that his life and legacy became the ground out of which the rest of Charlotte's life would be shaped. Significantly, it has become a life shaped by love, generosity, meaningful work, and social activism.

Our culture has a long tradition of separating work from play, profession from recreation. We draw arbitrary boundaries around our work lives, sometimes thinking that it protects our loved ones from stress, sometimes to protect ourselves from the stress. Yet our work, whether we run a company, drive a bus, make a quilt, cook a meal, or clean a hotel room, is a reflection of the presence or absence of meaning in our lives.

Although it may seem far-fetched, when we clean a hotel room or a home, we participate in an ancient ritual that honors the sacred nature of a human being; and cleanliness is placed next to holiness. In tribal and nomadic cultures, for instance, cleanliness and beautiful surroundings are part of daily life. The dirt floor is swept; art is carved or painted on the mud walls. Often when the conditions are most challenging and sparse, the people are colorful in dress and jewelry. They themselves bring beauty to their austere surroundings.

In Tibet, in Navajo country, in India, the brilliant dress and vibrant jewelry worn by "impoverished" people celebrates the deep meaning in their lives as well as their awareness of their "riches." It's interesting that in the 1980s in the United States, when commercial wealth was on the rise, the grunge movement became an expression of young people. Perhaps there is a kind of freedom in having little in the way of material possessions that liberates us to celebrate ourselves more deeply. Perhaps material excess, which in many ways is closely associated with both the will to pleasure and the will to power, hinders our ability to celebrate our spiritual awareness and the inherent beauty and meaning in our lives.

In the Buddhist tradition, the cook and the temple cleaner may be the most important teachers in the community. They are honed by their humbleness and by their attention to the details of daily life. Their attention creates meaning, and it is this—not their talks and teachings—that draws students to them. Sometimes the cook and the cleaner appear as Buddhist jesters, playing with their humble roles, hiding behind them, watching for ripe students to come their way. They are cleaners and cooks in waiting. If you talk to those in the service professions about their work, their stories will often amaze you. They see things that the rest of us don't. They experience human nature, often from behind a mask of professional detachment, in ways that most of us rarely have the chance to do.

Searching for Financial Independence

These days we are used to thinking about financial independence as the pathway to freedom. A few years ago an advertising campaign in Canada called Freedom 55 promised not only financial independence beginning at age fifty-five but also the lure of freedom to do whatever you would want for the rest of your life. With the average life span increasing for both men and women, I wondered what this kind of freedom would ultimately mean for such young retirees. What would they do with—and for—the rest of their lives?

At the same time, I came across evidence that older Canadians were spurning retirement, choosing the office and meaningful work over 24/7 bridge and golf—and not necessarily because they had to. Such older workers, in fact, may be offering aging baby boomers a peek into their own futures. In a 1998 survey of boomers sponsored by the American Association of Retired People (AARP), some 80 percent said that they would keep working beyond traditional retirement age. Although the reasons for working beyond traditional retirement age are many, including the influence of the economy at any given point, here is what one older worker had to say: "It's important to stay busy, to have goals and plans. There are still plenty of depressed retired people who have nothing to do. It's like they're waiting to die, and it's such a waste."[40]

Once again, we are reminded of the many twists and turns that occur naturally, although not always seamlessly, as we explore the labyrinth of meaning in our personal and work lives. The metaphor for freedom is also true in another important respect. Living and working from the inside out is a choice, both of attitude and action. As we learned in the previous chapter, true freedom is not "just another word for nothing left to lose," as the late singer Janis Joplin once suggested in song lyrics written by Kris Kristofferson. Whether we like it or not, we are not only free to choose but also responsible for our choices. So if we decide to put our real aspirations—whether they are personal or work-related—in a lockbox with the expectation that someday we'll return to fetch them, that's our choice. And, just as important, we must be prepared to live with the fact that we may never return to the contents of our lockbox, nor fully realize our will to meaning!

Going Inward

As prisoners of our thoughts, we can't always see very clearly through the bars of our metaphorical prison cell. To see more clearly, we must be willing to go inward:

> *It's time to go inward, take a look at myself.*
> *Time to make the most of the time that I've got left.*
> *Prison bars imagined are no less solid steel.*
>
> Rodney Crowell[41]

We frequently miss opportunities to enjoy the spaciousness that already exists within us to feel authentic meaning in our lives and work. Frankl would say that only if we remain aware of and committed to meaningful values will we be able to fully enjoy this spaciousness. Yet how can we ensure that we will remain aware of such important values in our lives? Let me now introduce you to two simple exercises that you can use for such a meaningful purpose.

The first exercise is based on Frankl's invitation, in his book *The Doctor and the Soul*, to spread our lives out before us like a beautiful mountain range. My version of the Mountain

Range Exercise goes like this: First, ask yourself (and feel free to invite your associates to participate) to look out over your personal or work life as one would look out over a mountain range. Whom would you place on the peaks before you? In other words, who are the people who have most influenced your personal life or your career and work life? These people may include authors, teachers, employers, leaders, or people in your personal life who have mentored or loved you, or whom you have loved or admired. You can use paper, colored pens, or markers to sketch out your mountain range and write on the peaks the names of the people who have influenced you.

Then look for recurring values—that is, values that surface as "influencers" more than once. For instance, you might recall the empowerment of a particular teacher or supervisor. Explore the key values of the various people who had contributed significantly to your personal or work life. Focus on those that you may have incorporated into your own value system. Which of these values are the most positive, the most meaningful? To which of these values have you been most committed over the course of your life and work? To which of these values are you most committed now?

As you can see, the Mountain Range Exercise helps you look at your personal life and work life from a different perspective. Through it you can discover recurring values, recognize your own uniqueness, and broaden your view about your work and personal lives. It is also an unfolding exercise, a new way of looking at life that can help you discover the essence of your will to meaning in life and work.

The second exercise is a little different, although it seeks to accomplish similar aims as the Mountain Range Exercise. I call this technique the Hero Exercise. First, jot down the names of three heroes. Based on your own definition of who or what constitutes a hero, this list might include people, animals (for instance, a pet), or even fictional or cartoon characters! The people or animals on your list could be alive or from some time in history.

Then for each of your heroes, list the key characteristics or attributes they possess that you admire. In other words, what is it about each of them that, in your view, makes them a hero? Now ask yourself: Which of these attributes do I possess or would I like to possess? Moreover, how do I or could I exhibit these qualities in my life?

I've done this exercise many times on my own, with other individuals, and with groups. Because the exercise doesn't define the notion of hero, everyone may use her or his unique definition of what constitutes heroism or being a hero. Whoever is chosen as heroes, it is the characteristics, attributes, or qualities identified through this exercise that are most revealing, memorable, and meaningful. The revealed qualities are almost always positive and inspirational, and, as in the Mountain Range Exercise, they identify those recurring values that are most important and meaningful to you. In group settings, I have also found these embedded qualities to be a source of resonance between the participants—a kind of spiritual glue—that helps to engage and connect people in meaningful ways.

Feelings of Inner Emptiness

In America we live surrounded by more material wealth than any other society in the world. Yet we are restless, unhappy, and disconnected, both from others and from our inner lives.

Suicide rates for young people are increasing, and the divide between those with wealth and those on the economic margins is growing. The state of the economy notwithstanding, we have the resources necessary for widespread health care and economic stability, as well as for dealing with the spiraling discrepancies between rich and poor, yet the value placed on money for its own sake is taking the place of respect for one another in particular, and for humanity in general.

> The truth is that as the struggle for survival has subsided, the question has emerged: survival for what? Even more people today have the means to live but no meaning to live for.[42]

These are dire times. Yet they were born of plenty. In his work, Frankl observed that as the struggle for basic physical survival of the human species subsided, the question that emerged is survival for what? Even as more people today have the financial means to live, they are struggling with the question, What are we living *for*? In the face of material abundance, our inner emptiness, or existential vacuum in Frankl's words, has become ever more pressing.

These observations were reinforced in an article that appeared in the *Utne Reader Online*, the Web-based medium of one of the best-known alternative publications in the United States. According to the authors, life in the postmodern world, especially in what they call "America the Blue," displays certain characteristics and influences that appear very much like manifestations of Frankl's existential vacuum:

> Why am I sad? Why am I anxious? Why can't I love? The answer, perhaps, lies deep in our collective subconscious. The route to the surface passes through the postmodern hall of mirrors. The trip looks forbidding. And yet it is a worthwhile excursion.

Think of it as trying to solve the tantalizing psychothriller of your own life, the ultimate existential whodunit. . . . Like it or not, we humans are stuck in a permanent crisis of meaning, a dark room from which we can never escape. Postmodernism pulls the philosophical carpet out from under us and leaves us in an existential void.[43]

Viktor Frankl, one of the world's most profound and true optimists, would disagree vehemently with the notion that we can never escape the dark room of meaninglessness. Perhaps postmodernism has fallen prey to its own beliefs, or lack thereof, in its nihilistic analysis, which basically devalues the meaning of all life. Postmodernism relies on modernism to lay claim to its own existence. For most of the world, modernism is still a dream—if, that is, modernism can be defined by such "modern" ideas as sufficient food and shelter. When we let ourselves be defined by the analytical arrogance of postmodern thinkers, injustice is served all around.

Frankl developed and practiced Logotherapy as a way to find and open the windows and doors of rooms of despair for everyone—from death-row inmates and the concentration-camp survivors to CEOs, cab or bus drivers, and postmodern philosophy professors. He designed a framework of being and doing that offers an entirely new design for our lives—rooms to live and work in that have both innate meaning *and* a view. He provided a disciplined approach for discovering meaning in even the most catastrophic of circumstances—an approach rooted firmly in his profound personal experience.

In addition to the feelings of inner emptiness that seem to exist among greater numbers of the working (and, for that matter, retired) population, more people feel trapped at work—and perhaps in life generally. How do employers and employees, as well as the citizens of the so-called free-agent nation,[44] deal with these complex issues? Unfortunately, many companies provide employees only with the illusion of feeling free and alive, as opposed to feeling trapped, at work. Even periodic pay increases and other financial rewards may only have this kind of illusory effect, especially if employers, albeit unconsciously, use such instruments in a way that fosters worker attention solely on the paycheck rather than on the reason(s) for their work. In this regard, it is perhaps worthwhile to point out that Frankl viewed the will to money as a primitive form of the will to power.

When he based his company's development on meaningful goals, Tom's of Maine founder Tom Chappell also brought deep personal meaning to his life. He created a company that invited all employees to share in a meaning-based bottom line. The company not only observed ethical environmental practices in the development of its products, it also gave 10 percent of pretax profits to addressing community concerns in Maine, its corporate base, and around the world. In addition, employees were allowed to spend 5 percent of their paid time volunteering. This commitment reflected more than traditional corporate social responsibility concerns; it encompassed ethical and soulful values that honor the emotional, intellectual, and spiritual life of both internal and external stakeholders, as well as the health and well-being of both the planet and the bottom line. In short, it is a partnership of meaning and a manifestation of what I call *meaningful capitalism*.

Let's look at another partnership of meaning in the corporate world, one that also transcends the traditional model of corporate social responsibility but in a very unusual way. Frank Stronach is the Canadian-based founder and chairman of Magna International, Inc., one of the world's largest and most diversified suppliers of automotive parts and systems. In addition to establishing a unique and meaning-focused corporate culture at Magna based on a business philosophy called fair enterprise, Mr. Stronach is well known for his entrepreneurial spirit and especially for his passion for Thoroughbred horse racing. He has purchased numerous racetracks across North America, including Santa Anita and Pimlico (home of the Triple Crown's Preakness Stakes), as well as has his own champion Thoroughbred racing and breeding operations in Canada and the United States.

Mr. Stronach immigrated to Canada from Austria (Viktor Frankl's homeland as well) at the age of twenty-two with nothing more than a suitcase and about forty dollars in his pocket. His humble beginnings and penchant for hard work helped to mold his character into a man who never forgot his roots. The same qualities served as the building blocks for his business acumen and, more fundamentally, for his orientation toward business ethics, corporate social responsibility, and accountability.

After Hurricane Katrina hit in August 2005, Mr. Stronach put this orientation to the test and at the same time realized his will to meaning: he convinced the American Red Cross to let him turn his Palm Meadows Thoroughbred Training Center, in Palm Beach County, Florida, into a shelter.

This upscale facility, which had been designed to house jockeys, trainers, and horses, soon became home to some three hundred "guests" (Stronach refused to refer to the victims as "evacuees," or even worse, "refugees"), many from the Lower

Ninth Ward of New Orleans, who had been randomly selected by the Red Cross and the Federal Emergency Management Agency. The point person for this relief effort was Dennis Mills, an executive at Magna and a former member of Canada's Parliament from Toronto for sixteen years. Among other things, Mills was a well-known catalyst for and orchestrator of major public events, such as the visit of Pope John Paul II to Canada for World Youth Day and the appearance of the Rolling Stones in Toronto for the successful SARS relief concert.

Mr. Mills, who is also a personal friend, is another reader of *Prisoners of Our Thoughts* who manifests the book's principles in his life and work. Given his long-standing commitment to public service, Dennis and I have discussed how to bring meaning-centered principles into the political arena to influence the formulation of public policy. Mills was an obvious choice to lead Magna's humanitarian initiative—he shared a will-to-meaning orientation with his boss and wanted to make a positive difference in the lives of the guests from New Orleans under their care.

A Bold Experiment

"Helping people, providing food and shelter, that's the easy part," Mr. Stronach said. "The challenging part is what do we do to get them back on their feet again?"

Enter Canadaville. Stronach purchased about a thousand acres of land northwest of New Orleans outside the hurricane zone, where families could start over and build a future. Canadian and U.S. flags fly side by side at the welcome center of this still-evolving community in rural Louisiana. Dennis Mills once again provided the leadership behind this extraordinary initiative on behalf of Frank Stronach and Magna, saying that "this is just neighbor helping neighbor." The residents at Palm Meadows had first dibs, but not all of them wanted to relocate to this planned community; some wanted to return to New Orleans, and some wanted to stay in Florida. Hence, Canadaville opened its doors to survivors from other shelters as well.

Those who chose to live at Canadaville could do so rent-free for five years as long as they followed a "charter of conduct." Among other things, this charter required that they work or go to school, volunteer at least eight hours a week, participate in the community council, and stay away from drugs. The community offers after-school and tutoring programs for children, computer and job-training classes for adults, and it operates an organic farm. And although Magna provides housing, health care, and other activities, residents do not receive cash payments: the purpose of Canadaville is to be a hand up, not a handout.

At this writing, Canadaville remains a work in progress as it continues to meaningfully engage and help those in need in the wake of Hurricanes Katrina and Rita. Frank Stronach and Dennis Mills exemplify authentic commitment to meaningful values and goals—the will to meaning—in the corporate world, providing inspirational role models for the moral transformation of capitalism. Let's hope that other business leaders follow their example.

The Cry for Meaning

But what about those of us who work in companies that are not as enlightened as Tom's of Maine or Magna? How do we acknowledge the ultimate worthiness of life in our work? If we step back from the superficial perspective of a job equals a paycheck, we can begin to search for meaning: How many opportunities do we have each day to connect meaningfully with others? Do we take those moments and make real contact? Do we honor the people we meet? Do we take the time to appreciate the power we have to bring meaning to our relationships? Do we honor our own time? Do we look for new, creative ways to perceive and approach our work? Are we experiencing our connections on many levels at once or are we limiting our experience to getting to the end of the day and the next paycheck? Metaphorically speaking, do we run from the parking lot to work each day or do we bless the moment when TGIF[45] arrives?

In his lectures and speeches, and in a book published initially in 1977, Frankl passionately warned about an "unheard cry for meaning." He characterized this cry as coming from a combination of depression, aggression, and addiction. These societal symptoms form what Frankl called a "mass neurotic triad"—what might now be dubbed a psychological axis of evil. It is a cry that needs to be understood in the context of the underlying existential void. This collective cry is perhaps more prevalent today than when it was first identified by Frankl, and it is not going away any time soon.

For instance, stress is killing us. Rage—road rage, airport rage, rage at work, school, home, even in the parking lot—has become a commonly defined social phenomenon. Going postal is a phrase all too common and all too peculiar to these times. We are becoming more and more cynical and skeptical about everything from corporate and governmental motives to the trustworthiness of our friends and neighbors. Educational systems are failing, and young people are becoming alienated and depressed. This collective unheard cry for meaning belies the mask of our have-a-nice-day culture. Only by hearing this cry, in our own voices and the voices of others, can having a meaningful day become the measurement of our daily life.

In his book *The Re-Enchantment of Everyday Life*, former Catholic monk and professor of religion and psychology Thomas Moore explores the possibility of experiencing enchantment at work. He writes about the Roman god Mercury, "the divine patron of commerce." In ancient Rome, business was considered sacred. Work, money, the arts, religion, and philosophy were integrated into daily life. Moore writes:

> *Economics is the law of life, and in fact this word also has deep meaning, coming from oikos, Greek for home or temple . . . and nomos, meaning management, custom and law. . . . Business involves all aspects of managing our home, whether the family house or the planet, and therefore has to do with survival, fulfillment, community, and meaning.*[46]

Finding enchantment at work might sound to some people like an exercise in futility, but it can and does happen. And when it happens, the ripple effect through the world of work can be monumental. To be enchanted means to be soulfully involved, to be beside ourselves with excitement, gratitude, appreciation—to be full of possibility. When we bring this meaning-focused sensibility to our work, creativity flourishes and so does productivity.

For example, take the case of Skaltek, a major equipment manufacturer based in Stockholm, Sweden. Listen to the words of Öystein Skalleberg, the founder of Skaltek, as he describes his philosophy about people and work:

> Every human being is a Leonardo da Vinci. The only problem
> is that he doesn't know it. His parents didn't know it, and they
> didn't treat him like a Leonardo. Therefore he didn't become like
> a Leonardo. That's my basic theory.[47]

Skalleberg practices what he preaches. At Skaltek, the company doesn't use job titles, avoiding conferring privileged status on certain people, and each employee's business card carries only pertinent contact information along with a photo. Once, when Skalleberg was asked about the policy on job titles, he responded that if he *were* to give his employees a job title, it would be something like Leonardo da Vinci or Unlimited Possibilities rather than the job titles used by most companies.

In addition, there are no cookie-cutter job descriptions, and all workers who help build a machine add their individual signature to the final product. In this way, there is not only a direct line from the customer to everyone involved in product development but also an emphasis on total quality management that is completely transparent. An even more radical practice at Skaltek is an annual employee appraisal process that involves the use of randomly selected performance review teams. According to Skalleberg, since no one knows who will be conducting their performance review each year, "Everybody smiles in all directions!" Skalleberg also has a revolutionary formula for building a company culture in the postmodern era: "*Confidence* is the start of it, *joy* is a part of it, *love* is the heart of it." Doesn't Skaltek sound like a company with a meaning-focused philosophy about bringing enchant-ment to work?

> *The salvation of man is through love and in love. I understood how a man who has nothing left in this world still may know bliss, be it only for a brief moment, in the contemplation of his beloved.*[48]

"An enchanted life is good for business, even if it requires a turnabout in values and vision," writes Moore.[49] His proof comes from evidence of the opposite perspective: the way the lack of enchantment in our work leads to emotional and physical distress, lowered morale, decreased productivity, and dispirited employees. In short, if we can't bring our soulful-ness to work, eventually we suffer. And so does business.

When there's soulfulness at the top of a company, the trickle-down effect can be explosive. In 1995, when fire destroyed the Malden Mills factory in Massachusetts, three thousand people were instantly out of jobs—but not for long. As he watched his factory burn, Aaron Feuerstein, president and CEO of the company, decided that it was not the end of Malden Mills. The first thing he did was keep all three thousand workers on the payroll with full benefits for three months. There was nowhere for them to work, but in his heart, mind, and soul he knew that it was unconscionable to put three thousand people out on the streets. The company was directly or indirectly involved on every level in the com-munity. It would be a death blow not only to the employees and their families but also to everyone in the cities of Law-rence and Methuen, Massachusetts. And because Malden Mills supplied high-tech fabrics for products sold by outdoor apparel retailers, such as L.L. Bean and Lands' End, his customers were at risk too.

It cost millions of dollars to keep all the workers on the payroll, and it put the company into bankruptcy, but Feuerstein prevailed. He risked everything—his money, his reputation, his business. He believed in his employees, and they in return believed in him. He set up temporary plants in old warehouses and the collective response was astounding.

"Before the fire that plant produced 130,000 yards a week," said Feuerstein. "A few weeks after the fire, it was up to 230,000 yards. Our people became very creative. They were willing to work twenty-five hours a day."

Feuerstein instinctively valued his workforce; he invested in their well-being immediately and with great risk. Then he put his will to the task of meaningfully rebuilding his company. It was the phoenix of possibility rising out of the ashes. The employees, blue-collar and white-collar alike, rose to the occasion and committed themselves to the collective good. In 2003, the company came out of bankruptcy.

When meaning is honored at the top of any organization, it can be easy to bring meaning to our jobs. It's a natural reflection of meaningful values. If we are valued and appreciated, if our well-being is nurtured, we feel a part of a meaningful whole. But soulfulness can trickle up, too. It might be more difficult to honor meaning at work with little evidence from above, but it also might be more important to do so.

There is an international crisis of corporate accountability. In many companies, there is no trickle-down soulfulness because the forces operating the companies are so distant and diffused that there can be no meaningful link down through the ranks. The financial bottom line becomes the only thing that defines meaning, and when this happens the ethical and moral decisions that are at the heart of capitalism are obliterated. They have to come from all of us as individuals, no matter what our roles are. The events on Wall Street and Main Street in America, along with those witnessed across the global economy at the end of the first decade of the new millennium, point to a desperate need for a moral transformation of capitalism—meaningful capitalism—if we ever expect to see the heart of capitalism beat again.

When we choose meaning in the workplace, we pay attention to everything around us. We choose respect, kindness, and courtesy. We choose justice and fair play. We bring our own ethical and moral decision making to our jobs, and we find ways to make an impact. Sometimes it might be by simple recognition of our co-workers; sometimes by writing a letter expressing our observations and concerns; sometimes through organizing support for a constructive change. Most of all, by understanding that when we ourselves bring meaning to work, we bring with us the possibility of meaningful change in the workplace and in the world around us.

A financial bottom line is not motivated by ethical and moral decisions; *people* are motivated by ethical and moral decisions. When people are replaced by money as the presiding force behind decision making—that is, the will to money or power—we have no choice but to become aware of the implications and do something about it. The most important thing we can do is to bring meaning out into the light. By refusing to be held prisoners of our thoughts, we can bring our will to meaning to work, and our work will mean something.

Meaning Moment Recall a situation in your personal life or work life in which you were challenged to examine your commitment to meaningful values or goals (this may even be your situation today). Perhaps you were faced with a job assignment that wasn't in alignment with your personal values. Maybe you were just unhappy with the work that you were doing. Or perhaps you were faced with a family matter that tested your personal values. How did you first come to recognize this challenge? What, if anything, did you actually do about it? As you think about the situation now, what did you learn from it? In particular, what did you learn about your commitment to meaningful values and goals — that is, your will to meaning? In hindsight, what could you have done differently in this situation?

Meaning Question: How do you ensure that you remain committed to meaningful values and goals and thereby realize your will to meaning in your personal and work life?

FOR FURTHER REFLECTION

Think about the underlying values and goals that characterize your personal life and your work or workplace. In what way(s) do they reflect Freud's will to pleasure, Adler's will to power, and Frankl's will to meaning?

Realize Your Will to Meaning

Detect the Meaning
of Life's Moments

*Live as if you were living already for the second time and as if you had
acted the first time as wrongly as you are about to act now!*[50]

Michelle had recently celebrated her fiftieth birthday but
was not quite ready to admit that she had reached the half-
century mark and was dreading retirement age. In fact, she
was not happy and not inclined to celebrate anything in her
life. Twice divorced and the single mother of two Generation
Xers, Michelle's personal life, as far as she was concerned, left
much to be desired. She didn't feel much better about her
work life either. Since her last marriage ended, she had been
having a very difficult time holding any kind of steady employment. Whenever she did find a job that seemed worthwhile,
it always soured quickly. Over and over, Michelle would find
herself stressed out at work, always for some reason that had
nothing to do with herself—a poor boss, lazy co-workers,
unclear job description, lack of support, and so on. Consequently, she was never satisfied with her work situation and

certainly never imagined that she could have a meaningful career path.

Because she was also stressed out at home, Michelle was experiencing a double whammy, with no end in sight. She seemed consumed by a need to put out fires at work and at home, with nothing in reserve for determining the root causes of her anguish. As she grew increasingly depressed over her life situation, Michelle's tendency to externalize the reasons for her plight hardened into a fixed habit. Michelle became oblivious to her own role and responsibility—as cocreator of her miserable reality—and effectively lost touch with the meaning of life's precious moments because she was too busy complaining about what life was doing *to* her. In her mind, life had dealt her a bad hand, so there was nothing to do but bear the suffering and complain loudly enough so everyone around her—family, friends, co-workers—would hear her cries of pain.

"The meaning of it all is that there is no meaning," said the golfer Walter Hogan in the movie *The Legend of Bagger Vance*. Michelle would agree, for the search for meaning had no value to her. Her life was meaningless and would continue to be meaningless—unless some sort of miracle came her way—for she wasn't inclined to search for a different way. Perhaps Michelle was simply experiencing a midlife crisis. Whatever the reason, ironically Michelle had chosen to take an early retirement from life by giving up on her search for meaning.

In contrast, let's consider Adam, who wrote to me after reading *Prisoners of Our Thoughts* and was applying the book's principles in response to a major life/work transition. After thirty years as a corporate engineer, he suddenly found himself leaving a position he loved and moving to an area with literally no work for him.

Suddenly, he said, his life had no meaning, and he found himself suffering through months of "oh, poor me" thoughts that held him prisoner. After reading my book, he began to look at his situation as an opportunity rather than a problem. As a result, he began to reinvent himself to accommodate the new set of life circumstances he could not change. He developed the understanding that he *could* change the way he perceived and reacted to his new, discomforting circumstances.

Gradually, as his attitude improved, so did his disposition, his outlook on life and work, and his progress toward what for him was a completely new type of fulfillment and success. Adam attributed much of this change in perspective and behavior to his newly found appreciation for the potential for meaning that exists in all of life's moments, even those that are not particularly pleasant, welcomed, or expected. He came to realize that his former poor me thoughts would not resolve his predicament, and that he alone was responsible for discovering the seeds of meaning that existed in his life. Unlike Michelle, Adam was willing (and able) to assume full responsibility for his situation, and he refused to take an early retirement from life by giving up on his search for meaning.

Sometimes it is the gravity of the hardships or challenges we face that forces us to detect the meaning of life's moments. After waging a courageous, year-and-a-half-long battle with pancreatic cancer, Patrick Swayze, an actor and classically trained dancer whose leading roles in the blockbuster films *Dirty Dancing* and *Ghost* made him a popular movie star, died on September 14, 2009. He was fifty-seven years old. "I'm proud of what I'm doing," Swayze had told the *New York Times* in October the year before, when he was still filming *The Beast*, an A&E television series in which he starred as an unorthodox FBI agent. "How do you nurture a positive attitude when all the statistics say you're a dead man? You go to work."

I have always admired Patrick Swayze, both as an actor and as a person, and found him to be an inspiration for others. In addition, I've felt a kinship with him for many years because we shared a passion for horses and for the martial arts. Interestingly, Swayze and his wife of more than thirty years, Lisa, owned a ranch not far from my home in Santa Fe, New Mexico, where they lived part-time. Here, to the Land of Enchantment, was where Swayze came when he wanted to get some true peace and quiet, as well as reflect upon the deeper meaning of his life beyond the celebrity spotlight. "I fell in love with New Mexico when I was shooting *Red Dawn*," he once told *Variety* magazine. "It's my healing place." The Swayzes even renewed their wedding vows at their New Mexico ranch in May 2008. This precious and priceless "meaning moment," I should add, took place in the midst of their campaign to overcome the deadly disease that was attacking Patrick's body.

We all know people, often people close to us, who have passed on. We may even have experienced the death of loved ones who have battled terminal illnesses such as pancreatic cancer, for which no cure exists. And if we are fortunate, we may know people like Patrick Swayze, who were inspirations and role models in ways that are not always easy to describe.

Despite personal hardships and formidable challenges, these people represent human beings at their best, even as conditions are worst. Observing them, we bear witness to the resilience and unlimited power of the human mind and spirit, and we come to better understand how the search for meaning is the primary intrinsic motivation of all human beings.

Finding Meaning

We don't create meaning—we find it. And we can't find it if we don't look for it. Meaning comes in all shapes and sizes. Sometimes it looms big in our lives; sometimes it slips in almost unobserved. We might miss a meaningful moment entirely, until days, months, or even years later what once seemed insignificant is revealed as a pivotal, life-changing moment. Or it might be the collective meaning of many moments that finally catches our mind's eye, as if we weave together a living quilt from moments that by themselves passed unnoticed.

Although we are not always aware of meaning, Frankl would say that it is present in every moment, wherever we go. All we have to do, in daily life and at work, is to wake up to meaning and take notice:

> The true meaning of life is to be discovered in the world rather than within man or his own psyche, as if it were a closed system.[51]

This sounds easy, but these days it can feel almost impossible to do. Our sound-bite society speeds up reality to such an extent that stopping to smell the roses seems archaic, like a sentimental activity from an earlier era. We have forgotten how to slow down and reflect. We're more likely to use a cell phone, check e-mail, or tweet something insignificant. Time is getting away from us, and so is meaning, and we notice both only when there isn't much left. We wake up one day, or don't sleep one night, and suddenly our exhaustion, the fragmentation of our lives, the unrelenting pace, leaves us bereft of meaning. What is it all about? We wonder.

We cannot answer the big question unless we discover answers to the smaller ones: What are we doing? Why are we doing it? What do our lives mean to us? What does our work mean? Every day our lives are rich with meaningful answers, but only when we stop long enough to appreciate meaning will it bloom in our lives. We have to really be there to detect and know meaning, and most of the time we are on our way somewhere else. The frenzy of activity at work and at home is challenging the very nature of our existence. If we don't stop long enough to search out our own existence, meaning will recede to an impossible dream.

But before we go on the hunt for meaning in life and at work, we need to know what meaning is. Meaning is simply the rhythm of life on earth—the tides, the stars, the seasons, the ebb and flow of life, the miraculous beingness of it all—and it is available to us at every moment, with no exceptions. Every astronaut who returns from outer space attests to the great miracle that is life on this earth. They have seen the planet suspended in the vastness of space, its continents and clouds luminous in an unfathomable universe, all life hanging by some invisible thread of possibility. Their jobs take them to cosmic heights, yet it is being back on earth that brings them to their knees.

The thirteenth-century Sufi poet Rumi writes, "It's never

too late to bend and kiss the earth." The meaningfulness of life, as we know it and don't know it, is manifest everywhere on this fragile planet. Wherever we are and whatever we do, it is this very existence of life that calls us to meaning. How are we inviting life into our lives? How are we bending and kissing this earthly experience? How are we acknowledging meaning in our lives, through our work, at our jobs? The answers are as varied as our needs.

Meaning is *not* found only in professional credibility, and making such distinctions is artificial and unnecessary. Our entire lives are rich with meaning, and therefore everything we do has meaning. We are free to make decisions out of love for whatever is in our hearts. When we stop to look at the reasons for our decisions, we will always find meaning. But it takes time to reflect, and even though there's as much time as ever, it seems as if less and less is available to us. Taking time back is the first step in opening ourselves to meaning. But first we must ask, Where does all the time go?

To begin with, technology is a great thief of time. I confess to remembering the time before telephone answering machines. People either reached one another or they didn't. There were no cell phones, no e-mail, or voice mail. People at home and at work took messages and left notes—on paper! As a result, there was spaciousness to decide when, and even whether, we returned calls, room to think, to consider, and to contemplate decisions—both simple and complex.

Over the past thirty years, the entire way we work and communicate has changed. If we don't respond instantly to an e-mail, phone call, or a "chat" message, it can seem tantamount to personal betrayal or professional ineptitude. Technology, which is supposed to make life easier, has added a new layer of obligations. If we're not careful, it controls us.

Of course, technology has a positive side: a revival of the written word via e-mail; access to enormous amounts of information via the Web; near-instant connectivity with family, friends, colleagues, and strangers via various social and professional networking platforms; greater accessibility via cell phones in emergencies; and, thanks to voice mail, no more important messages missed. But unless we set some limits, there is nowhere to hide from it all.

I know many people, including family members, friends, and colleagues, who are completely addicted to cell phones, especially so-called smart phones. They take a phone everywhere: on walks, shopping, driving (even where it is against the law), to restaurants, and, yes, to the movies, where, regrettably, they often forget to turn it off. The cell phone, with its many features, functions, and applications, seems to function as an appendage of their body, providing them with a reassuring symbol of their place in the world. "Can you hear me now?" has become a mantra for their lives. And while they remain "connected," an unintended consequence of this technology is that we are forced to listen to conversations we don't need or want to hear.

What about our reliance on e-mail and instant messaging as ways of staying connected and, more insidiously, obligated? How many people do you know who can't imagine a day without checking their e-mail or Twitter account? I suspect this is true of more and more of us: we are linked to outside obligations in ways that define much of our time. There is great possibility in this and also a great burden. It's extremely important that we recognize the difference and know when we are responding in ways that undermine our connection to meaning.

The Importance of Awareness

Everything comes down to awareness. It has been said that "it is more important to be aware than it is to be smart."[52] To be aware is to know meaning. To be aware takes time. If our lives are dominated by messages piling up or passive preoccupation with television or the Web, we lose out on meaning. We must be aware—see, hear, smell, touch, and taste the world—to find the meaning in our lives.

> All that is good and beautiful in the past is safely preserved in that past. On the other hand, so long as life remains, all guilt and all evil is still "redeemable.". . . This is not the case of a finished film . . . or an already existent film which is merely being unrolled. Rather, the film of this world is just being "shot." Which means nothing more or less than that the future—happily—still remains to be shaped; that is, it is at the disposal of man's responsibility.[53]

There are as many shades of meaning as there are colors. And nobody can determine meaning for someone else—detecting the meaning of life's moments is a personal responsibility. Like it or not, if we are aware that we're in a lousy job but we need to pay the rent, the job has meaning. We needn't resign ourselves to a lifelong lousy job, but there is meaning in the one we have right now. If we hate our boss because she's demanding and unappreciative, we can either be demanding and unappreciative right back or try to discover a life lesson in our predicament. Maybe the boss is trying too hard to succeed; maybe we're hearing a parental voice from our past rather than the boss; maybe we have an opportunity to practice our diplomatic skills with a difficult person. Or perhaps we are in a job that is not right for us!

In *Man's Search for Meaning*, Frankl describes a case in which he met with a high-ranking American diplomat at his office in Vienna, presumably to continue psychoanalytic treatment that this person had begun five years earlier in New York City.[54] At the outset Dr. Frankl asked the diplomat why he thought that he should undergo analysis—why it had started in the first place. It turned out that this patient had been discontented with his career and had found it difficult to comply with American foreign policy. His analyst, however, had told him again and again that he should to try to reconcile himself with his father, because his employer (the U.S. government) and his superiors were nothing but father figures. Consequently, his dissatisfaction with his job was due to hatred he unconsciously harbored toward his father.

For five years, the diplomat had accepted this interpretation of his plight, and he became increasingly confused—unable to see the forest of reality for the trees of symbols and images. After a few interviews with Dr. Frankl, it was clear that the diplomat's real problem was that his will to meaning was being frustrated by his vocation and that he actually longed to be engaged in some other kind of work. In the end, he decided to give up his profession and embark on another one, which, as it turned out, proved to be very gratifying to him. His anguish had been not because of his father but because of his own inability to choose work that had true meaning for him. If we allow ourselves to be aware of the many possibilities, we open ourselves to meaning.

We must also open ourselves to our own integrity and

authenticity, which is akin to living and working with meaning. Unfortunately, we are not always supported for searching for our authentic selves, especially in the workplace. The roots of this complex issue run deep into the soil (and soul) of the postmodern culture. Our integrity, our search for deeper purpose and meaning can take a bruising when held up against the search for more and more money. It's important to know what we are up against when we decide to take the time to become aware and to contemplate the meaning of meaning in our lives.

Living with Awareness

It is life itself that invites us to discover meaning, and when we live our lives with awareness, we express meaning in everything we do. *Webster's New International Dictionary* lists more than twenty definitions for the word *work* and more than a hundred other words or phrases that begin with the word *work*. But it's the first definition, with its two small root words, *to do*, that illustrates the meaning of them all. Whatever we *do* has meaning, whether it's a workout or a work of art.

> *Life retains its meaning under any conditions. It remains meaningful literally up to its last moment, up to one's last breath.*[55]

Knowing *why* we do things, however, is essential and is the beginning of real freedom and meaning in our lives. If we delve deep enough, we'll reach the two things that motivate us most: love and conscience. Frankl described these as intuitive capabilities: things we do without thinking, things that define us at our deepest level. "The truth," he wrote in *Man's Search for Meaning*, "is that love is the ultimate and the highest goal to which man can aspire."

It's not always easy to trace where love and conscience come into play in our lives, but if we stop to explore our decisions, they surface: We work nights so we can be with our kids in the morning and see them off to school. We grow vegetables organically to provide healthy food for the community. We operate a small business that offers employment to three people year-round in a difficult economy. We write poems to encourage family and friends. We consult with others to help them cope with stress. We teach sailing to inner-city kids. We manage a corporation with an emphasis on fair wages for workers abroad. We make quilts for families who are homeless. We work at a job we don't love because it gives us money to do something we do love. We organize to bring affordable housing to our community. We donate a thousand dollars to a local charity. We put a dollar in an outstretched hand. We build energy-efficient straw-bale houses. We wait tables so we can be onstage, raise our kids, feed our dog, pay the light bill. It all comes down to love and conscience. And when we see how our world is connected in this way, we can name why and know meaning.

Do you remember Öystein Skalleberg's revolutionary formula for building a company culture from chapter 5? Here it is again: "*Confidence* is the start of it, *joy* is a part of it, *love* is the heart of it." How many organizations, in any sector or industry, do you know that place the notion of love (not romantic love) at the heart of their operating credo? Now you know why the Skaltek work environment is unique and why Skalleberg's formula is so revolutionary.

The world is full of good deeds and the opportunity to do good deeds. When we don't do them, it's often out of fear of losing something: our status, a loved one, a job, security, our sense of identity, our place in the world. The notion of fear at work and in the workplace has received considerable attention over the years. In fact, driving fear out of the workplace has long been a core principle of total quality management, but it remains a formidable goal that has yet to be reached.[56] Against this backdrop, approaches that help individuals work through fear and help executives and managers become fearless are readily available to meet this challenge.[57]

In the 1991 film *Defending Your Life*, director/writer Albert Brooks plays Dan Miller, a successful business executive who takes delivery of a new BMW and plows it into a bus while trying to adjust the CD player. Dan finds himself dead but awake in a place called Judgment City, a heavenly way station that film critic Roger Ebert described as "run along the lines that would be recommended by a good MBA program." It is in Judgment City's courtroom where Dan must try to explain and defend his life, particularly those moments, shown on video, when fear was most evident in his actions. Consider the following dialogue, which takes place between Dan and his defense attorney, Bob Diamond (played by Rip Torn):

> *Bob Diamond:* Being from earth as you are and using as little of your brain as you do, your life has pretty much been devoted to dealing with fear.
> *Dan Miller:* It has?
> *Bob Diamond:* Everybody on earth deals with fear. That's what little brains do.
> ...
> *Bob Diamond:* Did you ever have friends whose stomachs hurt?
> *Dan Miller:* Every one of them.

Detect the Meaning of Life's Moments

Bob Diamond: It's fear. Fear is like a giant fog. It sits on your brain and blocks everything. Real feeling, true happiness, real joy, they can't get through that fog. But you lift it and buddy, you're in for the ride of your life.

What lessons about detecting the meaning of life's moments can we find in this dialogue? For one thing, fear is depicted metaphorically as the fog that blinds one in the search for meaning. In this context, fear relates to our inability to actualize creative expression, to experience new situations and relationships with others, and to change our attitude toward something or someone. According to Frankl, these are all sources of authentic meaning. To find authentic meaning in our lives, we need courage, which is not the absence of fear but the willingness and ability to walk through the fear—to tread, if you will, into the darkness of life's labyrinth of meaning. And it is during the worst times, including hardship and suffering, that our courage is put to its greatest test.

Over and over, we learn from those who have lost everything that the worst times are often the catalyst for the best times. What we learn from Viktor Frankl's life and work is that even the most profound grief and intolerable circumstances can open us to meaning. And so can the smallest moments. All we have to do is take back the time in our lives, pay attention to the details and know why.

> In the concentration camps, . . . in this living laboratory and on this testing ground, we watched and witnessed some of our comrades behave like swine while others behaved like saints. Man has both potentials within himself; which one is actualized depends on decisions but not on conditions.[58]

Searching for Meaning After Midlife

Sometimes we have to approach the search for meaning from another perspective. We have to know we don't know and start from there. We have to let meaning find us. This seems to be difficult as we grow older, especially at midlife, when we may encounter a critical crossroads on the path to meaning. Rather than having a so-called midlife crisis, writes Mark Gerzon in his book *Coming into Our Own: Understanding the Adult Metamorphosis*, we can begin a search for deeper love, purpose, and meaning that becomes possible in life's second half.[59] Envisioning life, including our work life, as a quest, not a crisis, after midlife is an opportunity that holds great power for all of us, including the baby boomers on the horizon of old age.

As life expectancy and leisure time increase in retirement years, people begin to ask the existential question, Is that all there is? Also, more people are retiring at an earlier age, some voluntarily, others forced into retirement through downsizing, mergers, and the like. The increased time becoming available to people under these scenarios means more people are becoming aware of meaning-centered questions. Even the stories of "retired" thirty-somethings from Silicon Valley—obviously rare now due to shifts in economic conditions—illustrate the dichotomy that can exist between success and fulfillment. Isolation, depression, and other symptoms of these lost souls among the nouveau riche appear to run counter to conventional wisdom. How could monetary wealth—and the time to do whatever you would want—be associated with a lack of personal meaning?

Retirement at later stages of life demands similar attention to questions of meaning, especially because of the extended life expectancy that workers in Western society now enjoy. Why is it, for instance, that some workers seem to retire from life while others redesign themselves for new and meaningful challenges in living and working? The life and legacy of Viktor Frankl have taught us to approach the aging process from a position of personal strength and in a way that respects the dignity of the human spirit. The post-midlife years of Frankl, who had not retired at over ninety years of age, provide a window for us to see how important the will to meaning can actually be throughout one's lifetime.

All things being equal, I suspect that the new "balanced scorecard" of the twenty-first century will be concerned more with success at making a life than with success at making a living. As people become aware of their mortality and their commitment to meaningful values and goals—that is, their will to meaning—they will be more likely to consider the kind of personal legacy they would like to leave behind. To Frankl, this kind of questioning is a manifestation of being truly human: "No ant, no bee, no animal will ever raise the question of whether or not its existence has a meaning, but man does. It's his privilege that he cares for a meaning to his existence. He is not only searching for such a meaning, but he is even entitled to it.... After all, it's a sign of intellectual honesty and sincerity."[60]

Drafting Our Legacy

By reflecting upon our existence and seeking to detect the meaning of life's moments, we also create the opportunity to draft our personal legacy, albeit as a work in progress. A number of simple, practical exercises can be used for this purpose; let me introduce you to some of them. Because I am blessed with living in the mountains of northern New Mexico, I like to call the first exercise High-Altitude Thinking.

Imagine that you are sitting high on a mountain peak overlooking your life. From this distance, you can see all of the roads you have taken, all of the stops you have made, all of the people you have encountered, all of the things you have done or experienced in your life. Like a mapmaker, draw the map of your life, using various symbols to highlight the milestones in each of the above areas. Ask yourself the significance or meaning of each milestone. Next, weave together the pieces of your life's map, referring to the milestones as the fabric to be used, and create a quilt that symbolizes your life and work. Embedded in your life/work quilt are the threads of your personal legacy.

The Obituary Exercise can also be used as a catalyst to reflect on your life, including your work life, and help you chart your path to a meaningful existence, though it takes a much different approach. Like Albert Brooks's character Dan Miller in the movie *Defending Your Life*, imagine that you have died. However, rather than imagining yourself in Judgment City, put yourself in the position of having to write your own obituary for the local newspaper. What would you say? In other words, how do you want to be remembered? What are the most important things you experienced in your life? Because the newspaper editor has given you a one-page space limitation, your message must be as succinct as possible.

An alternative to the Obituary Exercise is the Eulogy Exercise, shown in figure 1 on the next page. In this exercise,

Eulogy Exercise

Are you living and working in such a way that the last comments about you, especially from your family, friends, business associates, and customers/clients, are really what you want to have said? Imagine now that you have passed on and have been given the opportunity to write your own eulogy to be read at your funeral. Go ahead, fill in the blanks!

We have gathered here today to say farewell to
_____. The world had a
great need for someone who _____
_____ and _____
was the right person to fulfill this need.

_____ was most fulfilled
when _____
_____
_____.

I believe _____ was put on
this earth to _____
_____
_____.

The world is a much better place because
_____ was here and
we will miss her/him forever.

Figure 1. Eulogy Exercise.

you are asked to fill in the blanks on the form, again making sure that the last comments about you, to be recited at your funeral, are really what you want said![61] You have been given the unique opportunity to write your own eulogy, so make sure that you incorporate the things that matter most to you. Did you live and work with meaning? Now assume that someone else wrote your eulogy. What would be different about it? Remember Scrooge's experience in the classic tale A Christmas Carol. What would happen in your encounter with the Ghost of Christmas Yet to Come, in which you get a glimpse of your destiny? How would people remember you, talk about you? Also keep in mind the fate of Scrooge's former business partner, Jacob Marley, who was damned to walk the earth for all eternity, never to find rest or peace, dragging the heavy chains of his own life's doing.

To avoid subconsciously building, link by link, the chains of one's damnation and thwarting a meaningful personal legacy, it is necessary to detect and remain aware of the meaning of life's moments. Otherwise, unless you have the good fortune like Scrooge of being visited by three ghosts in the night, it may be too late! Here is another simple exercise—I call it Existential Digging—that provides a quick and easy way to detect the meaning of life's moments in "real time."

Whenever you encounter an experience or situation that is especially challenging or that you would describe as a meaning moment in your personal or work life, I'd like you to ask yourself the following four categories of questions:

1. How did you *respond* to the situation or life experience? What did you do and think?

2. How did you *feel* about the situation or life experience? What kinds of emotions were stirred up as a result of the experience or situation?

3. What did you *learn* from the situation or life experience? What new knowledge, skills, or attitude do you now possess because of the experience or situation?

4. How will you *grow* from the situation or life experience? How will you apply what you have *learned* from the experience or situation, especially key learning about yourself, to and for your personal development?

By faithfully and authentically addressing these four levels of existential questions, I guarantee that you will engage in the systematic process of detecting the meaning of life's moments. And while you obviously cannot respond to the four questions for every moment of your life, I highly recommend that you try to address situations or life experiences that really matter—or should matter—in your personal life and work life. I also suggest that you maintain a journal or some other kind of record of this information so that you can periodically review your experiences and chart your progress in dealing with the meaning of life's moments. In other words, are you really growing and developing as a result of your learning from various life situations or are you repeating old patterns of thinking and behavior? Moreover, do you recognize any common threads of meaning that may help you weave your unique tapestry of existence?

These exercises can not only help you reflect upon your life and work but can also detect what is most meaningful to you. In all but the last exercise, you are being asked to step up in some way to see the big picture of your life. In the last exercise, you are being asked to dig deeply into your life situations and come to grips with how and why you respond the way you do. You may or may not like what you see. Yet these exercises can give you the chance to consider your life's ultimate meaning, as Frankl would say. Whatever your religious or spiritual beliefs are, ultimate meaning is a metaphysical concept, one that clearly has its roots and values in spiritual matters. In his introduction to *The Doctor and the Soul*, Frankl wrote: "Life is a task. The religious man differs from the apparently irreligious man only by experiencing his existence not simply as a task, but as a mission." Now ask yourself: Is your life a task or a mission? What about your work?

As you map your life's path, write your obituary or eulogy, dig into your life experiences, draft your personal legacy, or piece together your life quilt, keep these life-affirming questions in mind. By remaining aware of the need to detect and learn from the meaning of life's moments, you ensure that you do not become a prisoner of your thoughts. And by focusing on meaning's big picture, while simultaneously seeking to notice life's meaning moments, your search for ultimate meaning begins and never ends.

Meaning Moment   Recall a situation in your personal life or work life when you were forced to deal with the fear of change (this may even be your situation today). Perhaps you were facing a change in lifestyle or relationship. Maybe you were facing a company downsizing or merger. Perhaps you were confronted with a new management style or the need for job retraining. Or perhaps you were facing retirement or another life transition. How did you first come to recognize the fear of change? What, if anything, did you actually do about it? As you think about the situation now, what did you learn from it? In particular, what did you learn about your ability to confront your fears and respond to change?

 Meaning Question: How are your life and your work like a mission rather than a series of tasks?

FOR FURTHER REFLECTION

Imagine that you have written your autobiography — with details about your life and work — and it is now on the *New York Times* best-seller list. What is the title of your autobiography? Name and briefly describe the chapters in your autobiography. Who are the people included in your acknowledgments section?

Don't Work Against Yourself

---

*Ironically enough, in the same way that fear brings to pass
what one is afraid of, likewise a forced intention
makes impossible what one forcibly wishes.*[62]

Have you ever worked so hard at something that the more
you tried, the harder the task became and the farther away
you seemed to get from your goal? In other words, one step
forward, two steps backward? I've experienced this kind of
situation in my life, including my work life. Let me share a
quick example that took place when I was a full-time professor, directing a graduate degree program in public administration at a university in the United States.

Among my duties as director, I was charged with the
challenge of obtaining accreditation from one of the discipline's professional associations. Becoming accredited was
viewed by those in the field as a prestigious distinction and
competitive advantage, through which my program stood to
gain increases in student enrollment, greater ease of faculty

recruitment, increased research funding, and other embellishments for its resource base.

I was also a new member of the faculty, so I took on the responsibility of seeking this accreditation milestone as a way of making my mark. As I moved full-steam ahead, demonstrating to all that I was committed and passionate, I was convinced that the objective would be reached in short order. The fact that I had been through this same accreditation process before at other institutions, I felt, was sufficient evidence that I knew what I was doing, and my experience would carry me through to another victory.

Alas, this did not turn out to be the case. I found pockets of resistance everywhere I looked, and the more I looked, the more resistance I found. My expertise in this process, I learned later, proved to be a liability. In this regard, because I *knew* what to do—and knew how to do it *best*—all of my colleagues were doing it wrong! I became fixated on every detail of the program, and I assured myself that I would be able to correct single-handedly any and all imperfections that might jeopardize the objective of gaining full accreditation.

I had good intentions, and most of my university colleagues, in hindsight, would probably agree with me. Unfortunately, my fixation on the outcome backfired, and I was unable to fulfill my ultimate goal. In fact, I never was able to obtain accreditation during my tenure as program head.

I could easily blame the situation on everyone else or at least shift to others the bulk of responsibility for failing to reach my objective. I choose not to do so, however, for now I can see how my own actions worked against me. I tried too hard to get everything done my way and, as a result, estranged myself from the very colleagues upon whom I depended for success. My fixation on the "right" way to do things, I have since learned, also had the effect of marginalizing their contributions to the process and, in some cases, even invited forms of subtle—if not overt—sabotage. Paradoxically, I had become my own worst enemy, and at the time I didn't even know it!

The meaning of life is meaning. The meaning of life *at work* is meaning. When we look for meaning, there is meaning in the looking. It's right here all around us, within us, and beyond us. But if we try too hard to create meaning, it can backfire, especially at work. Like our personal lives, our jobs come complete with their own dynamics. But unlike in our personal relationships, we can't always encounter our coworkers with emotional honesty and vulnerability. We think we have to be professional, we need to have professional goals and accountability. We have to perform.

> *Work usually represents the area in which the individual's uniqueness stands in relation to society and thus acquires meaning and value. This meaning and value, however, is attached to the person's work as a contribution to society, not to the actual occupation as such.*[63]

Sometimes our performance is measurable—what we produce might be immediately tangible: making sales or products, meeting a quota, driving a certain distance in a day, meeting a deadline, baking bread, fixing a car, or serving a customer. Other professional responsibilities are less tangible, involving long-term planning and projects that require creative involvement, teamwork, complex expectations, and more subjective goal setting. They all require performance and most often evaluation as well. In our jobs, most of us are accountable to others. We want to please, to perform well, and to be effective at what we do. And it's often when we most want to impress others that we undermine ourselves. Our thoughts go out beyond our situation; we become obsessed with results, and we overlook the very success we are searching for.

Relationships at Work

One reason we may miss succeeding is that we overlook the importance of relationships in the workplace. Our jobs are always more than just jobs. They represent relation-ships—with ourselves and co-workers; with customers and consumers; with the products we are designing, creating, and selling; with the services we offer; and with the environment and the ways in which our work affects the world. These rela-tionships weave together through our work, and they have meaning individually and collectively. When we focus too intently on outcomes, these relationships suffer. The harder we work for success, the more elusive it can become.

> The job at which one works is not what counts, but rather the manner in which one does the work.[64]

Angela had just graduated from college with a degree in business administration, and she was especially excited when she was promoted to a supervisory position at the drugstore where she worked. It was her first stab at being a manager, and she envisioned this promotion as her initial step up the corporate ladder. Of course, she wanted more than anything to do her best in the new job and prove to her bosses that they made the right decision in promoting her.

Right away, Angela proclaimed her intentions for building better teamwork, sharing responsibilities, and improving performance with all the employees on her shift. Her enthusiasm appeared to be contagious, and it looked as if she would be able to make some major improvements immediately. Because the drugstore was in my neighborhood and I was a regular customer, I had a chance to learn first-hand about the changes that were happening, directly from Angela.

"My co-workers are unbelievably lazy and don't carry their weight around here no matter what I say or do," she complained to me one day. I listened and left, assuming that she was just having a bad day. However, this proved not to be the end of the matter. From then on, every time I saw Angela, even if she wasn't complaining directly to me, I would overhear her complain to other customers about her problems at work. Indeed, she displayed an extremely negative attitude about work and was quick to point out the failings of other employees. In my view, her work situation had become dysfunctional and, from what I could tell, for reasons that were largely her own doing.

Angela had been exhibiting two behavioral traits or tendencies—*hyperintention* and *hyperreflection*—that are central to Viktor Frankl's teachings. Let me explain these concepts by using Angela as an example. Angela was unaware that she had begun to micromanage her employees in order to attain her goal of demonstrating that she was a good manager and could achieve her stated performance objectives. Unfortunately, she became so fixated on accomplishing her mission (that is, she was hyperintending) that she could see only problems (she was hyperreflecting), not the solutions to her escalating management dilemma. Paradoxically, the more she complained and called for increased teamwork, job sharing, and improved performance, the less she saw among her co-workers.

Moreover, Angela had become so consumed with her intended outcome—a form of anticipatory anxiety—that she began to see herself failing to achieve it, which was evident in her negative attitude about work. In effect, she had unconsciously created a self-fulfilling prophecy, as many of us do. Unfortunately, she was unaware that letting go of her intentions would probably have allowed her to find ways to resolve the situation and fulfill her original work objectives.

Paradoxical Intention

Meaning is found in the awareness of the moment, and when we move too far from the moment, we start to lose our effectiveness. Even when the stakes are high and our success essential, focusing on the results rather than on the process can prevent a successful outcome. We all know how it works: our nervousness and anxiety about getting it right keep us from getting it right. The higher our expectations are about something, the more disconnected we are from the actual process, and the less we are able to participate in the project's successful unfolding.

Frankl calls this *paradoxical intention*. Our good intentions actually become the cause of our failure. When a specific success is so fervently sought that we overlook and neglect the relationships that are an integral part of the process, we lay the seeds for something to go wrong. We fly in the face of our own success. We neglect our own meaning, the meaning of others, and the meaning of the process.

"My boss is a jerk." "My boss hates me." "My boss steals all the credit." How many times have you made or heard statements like these? Time out. Think about what you are saying, what it really means, and how it may be affecting you or your co-workers. Bosses do have flaws, and many of them are significant. On the other hand, most bosses are not the pointy-haired characters portrayed in Dilbert cartoons. They have usually moved up in the company or organization for a good reason. If you dismiss your boss because of flaws, you may be cheating yourself out of a chance to learn and grow.

Again, think about it: What is your boss good at? What can you learn from him or her? What kind of workers get along best with your boss? Are *you* doing anything that brings out the worst in your boss? From the perspective of Frankl's paradoxical intention, are you encouraging your boss, no matter how abusive he or she may be, to be a micromanager by asking questions every few minutes rather than by doing your job well? And then ask yourself if that is what you really want. If it's not, you might be working against yourself!

We are all intuitive; we are all affected by the moods of those around us; we all know feelings of trust and mistrust; we all know when something "just doesn't feel right." We recognize when we are being treated badly, superficially, carelessly, or dishonestly, whether in our personal life or our professional life. It is the quality of these interactions that create our relationships and our incentives to do our best.

We know when we are being used as part of someone else's agenda. We sense when our intrinsic meaning as a human being is being overlooked in the wake of somebody else's ambition. This is true of a top-level CEO or the new kid in the corner cubicle. When someone is so desperate to be recognized at work by a promotion or a raise, there is a general sense of artificial behavior. Interactions and atmosphere do not feel quite real. Something is missing, and it's usually meaning.

Consider Neal, a software engineer at a major high-tech firm. Newly married, Neal had just completed an MBA degree from a prestigious university and was determined to be promoted to a management position as quickly as possible. He was so determined to show off his newly acquired management knowledge and skills—primarily as a way to propel himself up the corporate ladder—that he went out of his way to be noticed by his supervisors, even if it meant ignoring or irritating his co-workers. Neal's technical skills as a software engineer were recognized, but his people skills were not. In fact, his co-workers did not consider him a team player, let alone a supervisor or leader, and they voiced their disdain for him whenever possible. At team meetings, during performance reviews, and around the watercooler, Neal the aspiring manager was targeted as out of touch with and was disliked by the very colleagues he had hoped to supervise.

Because Neal was so busy looking up at his prospects for promotion, he failed to see that the water was beginning to boil all around him! So, no matter how competent he depicted himself as a manager, and no matter how hard he tried to convince his bosses to promote him, he was unable to do so. He was fixated on the promotion, but the more he tried to get it, the farther out of reach it became! And because Neal was unaware of the meaning moments that begged for his attention, he was unable to adjust his course. All things considered, he was working against himself!

Whenever we overlook the opportunity to have respect-ful, meaningful moments with others at work, we undermine our chances of long-term success. And when we do take the time to nurture our relationships, the definition of success expands exponentially. Our day-to-day, minute-by-minute lives become successful in and of themselves, and our specific goals become more accessible.

In work relationships, it is important to recognize that business and personal issues are frequently tied together. "Smart companies know that the individual's ability to cre-ate relationships" is the engine that drives value.[65] Trusting each other's motives is also critical to success, both in the moment and over the long haul. If trust is missing, we can get caught up not only in figuring out how others are trying to undermine us but also in calculating how best to respond to their motivations. As a result, the search for meaning at work suffers, and the engine that drives value sputters or stalls.

The tendency to hold others, such as co-workers, prison-ers of your thoughts can also work in ways opposite to our intentions. For example, in their article "The Set-Up-to-Fail Syndrome," Jean Francois Manzoni and Jean-Louis Barsoux describe the way bosses often consign weaker performers to an "out-group" because they assume that these employees are less willing to go the extra mile, are more passive, and are less innovative.[66] This management approach, and the assump-tions upon which it is based, then becomes a self-fulfilling prophecy. Because they have been typecast as weak perform-ers and management has low expectations of them, these employees tend to allow their performance to erode to meet expectations. So even though the bosses sought to get the best performance possible through the out-group assignment, their personal attitudes and business decisions eventually worked against them.

How many of us have been terrorized by a micromanager, either in our personal lives or at work? You know, someone who doesn't have any trust in our ability to be responsible and productive? It is so disconcerting to be treated with such condescension. We may lower ourselves to fulfill the negative expectations to the absolute best of our ability. The opposite of micromanagers, who think their way is the only way, are missing managers who stay so far out of the picture they have no idea what goes on and have no effect on the success of the work group. Or how about those managers who profess to practice management by wandering around (MBWA): "Keep up the good work, whatever it is, whoever you are!" If the micromanager, the missing manager, and the pseudo-MBWA manager can stop long enough to honor the fact that the job means something to us, that we mean something to them and to ourselves, and that we mean well, progress is possible. If not, we are likely to hover in insecurity and indecision, which doesn't serve us, the manager, or the job.

These three different kinds of managers are seriously intent on success, but they all overlook the human beings in front of them. In doing so, they reduce their effectiveness on the job and ultimately limit, instead of developing, their success:

> For the dignity of man forbids his being himself a means, his becoming a mere instrument of the labor process, being degraded to a means of production. The capacity to work is not everything; it is neither a sufficient nor essential basis for a meaningful life. A man can be capable of working and nevertheless not lead a mean-

ingful life; and another can be incapable of working and nevertheless give his life meaning.[67]

When hyperintention gets in the way of progress, we sidestep meaning. When we sidestep meaning, we undermine relationships. When we undermine relationships, we put respect at risk. When there's not enough respect, there's not enough creativity and productivity. The tendency to set our sights beyond our situation can certainly establish a worthy goal initially. In the process of getting there, however, we have to let meaning lead the way.

And along the way, we have to trust in our own meaning. Few of us move through our lives unscathed. We get divorced; we lose our jobs, sometimes after many years of dedicated service; our health fails us in some way; our kids fail us; we fail one another. Life can be as full of failures as it is of successes. Yet in our failures we can find tremendous meaning, and only in meaning do our failures have a useful legacy. When our failures become useful, we triumph over them. Instead of leading with our disappointment and bitterness over a job loss or a lost relationship, we lead with our ability to have compassion and understanding—for ourselves and for others. Then, in our search for our next job, our next friend, we project wisdom and experience. Our appeal is heightened and our possibilities increase.

The power of failure has received an increasing amount of attention in the world of business, both in the literature[68] and among motivational speakers. Management guru Tom Peters, for instance, has advised that "only with failure can you verify wrong ways of doing things and discard those practices that hinder success."[69] Tales of failure that offer lessons of recovery and fighting back are being used by a new breed of speakers who are turning to the drama of defeat to inspire.

Paradoxical intention is more than a concept; it is a technique that Frankl developed and incorporated into his system of Logotherapy. The technique was used by Frankl as early as 1939 to help patients deal with a broad range of irrational fears and anxieties, as well as obsessive-compulsive behaviors. For example, by asking a patient who suffered from a phobia to *intend*, even if only for a moment, precisely that which he or she feared, Frankl observed dramatic results in reducing the phobia or eliminating it all together. In his words, when used effectively this technique "takes the wind out of the sails of the anxiety by reversing one's attitude and replacing a fear with a paradoxical wish."[70] Instead of fighting the fear, the person is encouraged to welcome it, even to exaggerate it. The person deflates the anxiety associated with the situation by no longer resisting it. Thus, ". . . while anxiety creates the symptoms over and over, paradoxical intention strangles them, over and over."[71]

Let me now describe some situations in which paradoxical intention either was used or may be appropriate. Frankl's writing provides many instances in which he used the technique with his patients. Two in particular stand out because they involve a work-related or workplace situation. In one case, the patient was a bookkeeper who was in extreme despair, confessing that he was close to suicide. For some years, he had suffered from writer's cramp, which had become so severe that he was in danger of losing his job. Previous treatments had been of no avail, and the patient was now desperate. Frankl recommended to the patient that he do exactly the opposite of what he usually had done—namely, instead of trying to write as neatly and legibly as possible (remember, this is before computers), to write with the worst possible scrawl. He was advised to say to himself, "Now I will show people what a good scribbler I am!" And at the moment that he tried to scribble, he was unable to do so. Instead, his handwriting was actually legible. Within forty-eight hours he had freed himself from his writer's cramp, was a happy man again, and was fully able to work.[72]

Another case involved a young physician who consulted Frankl because of his fear of perspiring. One day he had met his boss on the street and, as he extended his hand in greeting, noticed that he was sweating more than usual. This situation was aggravated as the physician's anticipatory anxiety increased with each new encounter. In order to break this cycle, Frankl advised him, if sweating should recur, to resolve deliberately to show people how much he could sweat. A week later he returned to report that whenever he met anyone who triggered his anxiety, he said to himself, "I only sweated out a quart before, but now I'm going to pour at least ten quarts!" Frankl writes that after a single session, the young physician was able to free himself permanently of the phobia from which he had suffered for four years.[73] And he no longer sweated abnormally when he encountered other people. One could imagine Albert Brooks, in his role as a newscaster in the movie *Network News*, employing paradoxical intention in the memorable scene where he is plagued with profuse and embarrassing sweating!

In his autobiography, Frankl recalled once using paradoxical intention to get out of a traffic ticket. He had driven through a yellow light and was pulled over by a police officer. As this officer menacingly approached him, Frankl greeted him with a flood of self-accusations: "You're right, officer. How could I do such a thing? I have no excuse. I am sure I will never do it again, and this will be a lesson for me. This is certainly a crime that deserves punishment." As the story goes, the officer did his best to calm Frankl; he reassured him that he need not worry—that such a thing could happen to anyone, and that he was sure he would never do it again. The technique worked, and Frankl was saved from getting a ticket![74]

Using Paradoxical Intention

So how might you use the technique of paradoxical intention in your own work and life situations? Basically, you first must be able and willing to shift your attitude about your situation (recall the discussion and exercises in chapter 4). This requires that you lighten up, tapping into your sense of humor, and let go in order to see the situation from a different perspective. In short, you need to be ready and able to plan for the fear or anxiety to happen rather than fighting or ignoring it. One exercise to help you with this process, called the Trash Can Exercise, is to first write down and then place your worries, fears, and obsessive-compulsive or other negative thoughts into a real trash can or box. Through this simple exercise, you will find that you have not only effectively identified your worst fears but have also decided to hold them consciously at bay by letting go of them. You can also design, as did Dr. Frankl with his patients, a plan that invites—and exaggerates—your worst-case scenarios into your personal or work life. Without necessarily implementing your plan, what does it suggest about your situation? What can you learn from it? What might you do with or about it?

> *Paradoxical intention is the exact opposite of persuasion, since it is not suggested that the patient simply suppress his fears (by the rational conviction that they are groundless) but, rather, that he overcome them by exaggerating them!*[75]

Meaning rests in appreciation of the moment, in gratitude, in awareness, and in relationship. When our awareness is focused only on the future, we lose all connection to now—where we are, where others are, and where the meaning is. When we don't appreciate the present, we aren't appreciating the process. When we aren't grateful for the meaning in our life right now, we aren't honoring ourselves or others.

Our lives have inherent meaning, no matter how we measure our success. And even when we do reach the pinnacle of professional success in some endeavor, the feelings that come with such success are fleeting. The goal is reached, now what? Suddenly there is a sinking feeling, emptiness settles in, and we wonder what it all really means. Is this all there is? If we have forsaken the means for the end, then the end really *is* the end!

Anybody who has accomplished a task at great cost to themselves in time, money, or energy will nearly always feel let down to some degree when the task is over. The engagement of our whole being in making something happen gives immediate purpose to our lives, and then it is gone. But the more meaning there is in the process, the more deeply satisfied we will feel, no matter what the outcome is.

When we treasure the process, the end becomes a new beginning. At work, when we pay attention to those around us and to the integrity of the process, we experience immeasurable success, no matter what the outcome is. By sustaining the awareness of meaning in our personal and work lives, we sustain the deeper feelings of success. And from this relatedness, other, more specific goals have the best chance of success.

When we stay true to our personal values in our professional lives, we lay a foundation of meaning. When we work in awareness of the moment, we stay connected to meaning. Our existence, and the existence of all life, is meaning. Meaning is simply waiting to be discovered, whether we work at a construction site, a bakery, a high school, a movie theater, a multinational corporation, a landfill, a restaurant, a home office, or the White House. By not being prisoners of our thoughts, and by not working against ourselves, we bring meaning to work.

Meaning Moment Recall a situation in your personal or work life in which the harder you worked to achieve an outcome, the farther away you seemed to be from your goal (this may even be your situation today). You know, the "one step forward, two steps back" kind of situation. Perhaps you were trying to develop a romantic relationship or a close friendship with another person. Perhaps you were seeking a promotion or were trying to get a creative idea or project approved by your boss. Or perhaps you were trying to finish a project, at home or at work, that seemed to have no end. How did you first come to recognize that you were not making progress? How did you rationalize or justify your dilemma? To what extent, if any, did you think or feel that you were partly to blame?

To what extent, if any, did you think or feel that you were working against yourself? What, if anything, did you actually do about it? As you think about the situation now, what did you learn from it? What could you have done differently in this situation?

 Meaning Question: How do you ensure that you don't work against yourself in your personal life and work life?

FOR FURTHER REFLECTION

Think about what it means to be aware of the connections you have with your family members, friends, and co-workers, including their feelings, and what it means for them to be aware of their connection to you and your feelings. In what way(s) might you strengthen and show that you treasure these connections?

Look at Yourself
from a Distance

*We know that humor is a paramount way of putting distance
between something and oneself. One might say as well,
that humor helps man rise above his own predicament
by allowing him to look at himself in a more detached way.*[76]

The ad in a London newspaper read, "Unemployed. Brilliant
mind offers its services completely free; the survival of the
body must be provided for by adequate salary." Viktor Frankl
quoted this ad in his book *The Doctor and the Soul* to make
an important point about the different ways in which people
may respond to being unemployed. Frankl was not suggesting
that unemployment is not a serious matter; on the contrary,
he emphasizes that being unemployed is a "tragedy because
a job is the only source of livelihood for most people." This
newspaper ad also reflects the fact that not all unemployed
people experience inner emptiness or feelings of uselessness
because they are unoccupied.

First, the fact that we do not have paid work does not
mean that life itself has no meaning for us. Second, our attitude toward any situation, including unemployment and

other major life challenges, determines our ability and willingness to respond effectively. The person who placed the ad turned a dire situation into something humorous because she was able to put distance between herself and the issue. She was able to look at herself from a distance as well, which allowed her to find meaning in her plight and take appropriate action to remedy the situation. Even the wording of the ad reflects her sense of humor and her innate, distinctly human capacity to look at herself in a detached way and rise above her predicament.

Humor and Cheerfulness

If there's one thing I wished I'd learned to do at a ripe young age, it's to laugh at myself more easily and more often. Growing up, I was a very serious person—uptight you might even say. In my early experience, having a sense of humor was more likely to get me in trouble—at home, in school, and at work—than it was to help me deal with life's transitions. I didn't learn to fully appreciate my sense of humor until much later in life, but it surely came in handy, especially during difficult times, after I learned how to use it effectively.

It might seem contradictory or at least a bit odd to write about humor in a book about meaning. But Frankl believed that a sense of humor is a trait that distinguishes us as humans. We all know dogs who smile—but they don't burst out laughing, especially at themselves, when they forget for the umpteenth time where they buried their latest bone! Humor about ourselves represents the essence of self-detachment, especially when the joke is on us (the late comedian Rodney Dangerfield built an entire career on his self-detachment). Humor and laughter tell us, and anyone within earshot, that we aren't tak-ing ourselves too seriously—and isn't that a relief? Our human ability to laugh at ourselves takes the edge off every serious work situation; and every serious work situation deserves, and needs, a dose of humor. We not only show others that we "don't sweat the small stuff" but we also show ourselves that we're no excep-tion to the principle of self-detachment.

The old joke goes: "Who ever lifted their head off their deathbed to say, 'Gee, I wish I'd gone to the office more often'?" To my knowledge, no one has—so far anyway. No matter how meaningful our work is, its meaning comes from our values, the deeper inclinations of our hearts and minds. Our jobs and work are part of our meaning; they represent our intentions to provide for our families, for ourselves, for our community, and for the world. But they are not who we are —they are what we do and how we do it. And when we can joke about what we do, in a paradoxical way we are taking seriously who we are.

An astonishing example of paradox is the Dalai Lama, the spiritual and temporal leader of the Tibetan people. He has witnessed the horrific genocide of his beloved people. Millions of Tibetans, including a large number of the spiritual community of Buddhist monks and nuns, have been tortured and murdered by the Chinese. Yet no one laughs louder at himself than the Dalai Lama. Nor do we often see happiness so gloriously displayed. He knows the tragedy of his time, yet he also knows happiness, humor, and lightheartedness.

In their book *The Art of Happiness at Work*, the Dalai Lama's coauthor, Howard Cutler, makes the following obser-vation about His Holiness:

At last things fell into place. I finally understood how the Dalai Lama could claim "I do nothing," as his job description. Of course, I knew that with his lighthearted humor, there was a tongue-in-cheek element to this job description. And behind his joking about doing "nothing," I knew of his natural reluctance, which I have observed on many occasions, to engage in unnecessary self-appraisal. This seemed to grow out of his lack of self-involvement, absence of self-absorption, and lack of concern for how others view his work, as long as he had sincere motivation to be of help to others.[77]

This is a great gift. And when we bring humor to our working world, it too is a gift. Humor is a great equalizer. It makes a CEO less intimidating and a cab driver more adorable, and the other way around. An adorable CEO can do more for morale than a big raise. A funny cab driver can lighten up an entire, responsibility-ridden day (if, of course, the driver gets you where you're going on time).

A sense of humor is usually accompanied by cheerfulness. Here's another of those misleading words. Most cheerful people I know have experienced real tragedy in their lives. When tragedy strikes, it takes us to the depths of grief. Going through grief brings us to cheerfulness. When we know how bad it can be, we find out, as the actor Jack Nicholson would say, how good it can get.

Cheerfulness is *not* "have-a-nice-day" artifice. It's a way of experiencing the present, no matter the weight of the world or the weather. Cheerfulness celebrates the possibility of finding meaning around every corner. It buoys us up beyond our individual concerns and invites us and others around us to find something to be happy about. This doesn't mean we hide behind cheerfulness. We simply lighten up and laugh.

A moment of humor at the right time can lift us out of

our self-imposed misery faster than anything else. When we detach ourselves from ourselves and our situation, we don't diminish or deny the circumstances—we go beyond them. We see, feel, and appreciate ourselves as separate from the distress; we accept and rise above.

Humor and Self-Detachment at Work

Let's consider some serious topics that have overshadowed corporate America the last few years: accounting fraud and the erosion of business ethics. What could possibly be humorous about the corporate crime wave, and how could a light-hearted approach be used to possibly improve the situation in the years ahead?

Andy Borowitz, a stand-up comedian and author of the book *Who Moved My Soap? The CEO's Guide to Surviving in Prison*, offers such an approach—one that balances laughter with serious introspection. Speaking at some of the premier business schools in America, Borowitz has shown that satire can be an effective, if offbeat, way to address the subject of CEO and corporate credibility. Getting business ethics into the open and addressing them humorously can be therapeutic for both individual business leaders and their organizations. Moreover, Borowitz has already found that his brand of humor can be a useful tool for advancing business education, complementing traditional courses in business ethics. After his presentation at the Wharton School (University of Pennsylvania), for example, one second-year MBA student said: "To be able to laugh and find some humor will likely help move us forward. There is still a crisis in how people view corporate leaders." And an incoming MBA student responded: "It was so refreshing. There was an underlying lesson of 'don't take yourself so seriously.'"[78]

People at work don't have to know the details of our lives; they just need to know a bit about the true meaning in our lives. When we are able to acknowledge our own meaning, we acknowledge the meaning in everyone else's life as well. Then we can detach ourselves from our difficulties, look at ourselves from a distance, and get on with the job, often with humor as our best friend.

In the world of work, emergency medical care workers have considerable experience with a particular kind of self-detachment. Their jobs, by definition, are pressure-filled, stressful, and meaningful. Yet they have to detach themselves from self and the situation facing them—often involving the life or death of the person in distress—in order to do their work effectively and with meaning. When it comes to humor, on any given day a roomful of emergency responders are much funnier than a barrel of stockbrokers on a good day. Humor supports the self-detachment necessary to maintain emotional distance from their patients, so they can observe themselves and their work from a distance to rise above and deal effectively with the stresses of the moment.

In the post–9/11 environment, communities nationwide are responsible for emergency planning for everything from fire and car accidents to bombs and bioterrorism. In one small county (in a southwestern state), dozens of people show up at a monthly meeting. The jobs represented include police, the fire department, emergency medical services, town, county, and state government, the National Guard, environmental groups, the Red Cross, ham radio operators, the health department, and telephone and power companies. For two hours, they discuss the direst emergency possibilities and how best to respond. There's a laugh a minute—at themselves and one another—along with the serious work that has to be done.

We never know what's really going on in people's personal lives. We do know that they include both challenges and rewards. Some co-workers may go home to isolation and loneliness, others to a happy family life. All experience both the joys and grief that life offers; they struggle with making ends meet, with teenage or small or no kids, with babysitters, aging parents, car payments, health-care expenses, and all the other demands of daily life. Every day, people around the world rise to the occasions in their life and go to work. They bring with them their entire lives, even as they focus on the work at hand.

Being able to detach ourselves from mistakes, our own and others', is another skill that's very useful at work. Nobody likes to make mistakes, but when we can acknowledge our mistakes, and laugh at them, it can be a huge relief for those around us. What are mistakes anyway but lessons to learn from?[79] And who hasn't felt stupid at work sometimes? It comes with the territory, with living. There's a saying that we're only as good as our mistakes, but first we have to acknowledge that we made them.

When someone comes to us at work and says "I made a mistake," most of us feel empathy. It takes self-detachment to own up to a mistake, to look at yourself and say, "I goofed," and then move on with your work and life. We are at the same time the person who doesn't want to make a mistake and the person who made a mistake. The person inside us who doesn't want to make a mistake is in the driver's seat almost of the time. But mistakes are momentary. When we dwell on our mistakes we give them far too much credit. When we acknowledge them and laugh them off, we reassure those around us that their mistakes, too, are momentary and not who they are. I'm reminded of a Calvin and Hobbes cartoon in which Calvin trips, flips, and falls down, only to get up with arms outstretched and say, "TA-DAAA!!!"

Of course, mistakes come in all shapes and sizes. The big ones might never be fuel for humor, but they are always life lessons that teach us humility and eventually, deep down, teach us meaning. They teach us that we are more than even our most terrible mistakes. If Viktor Frankl could find humor in concentration camps, perhaps there's no situation imaginable that couldn't somehow, at some moment, include humor.

In his writing and lectures, Frankl described a kind of cabaret that was improvised from time to time in the concentration camp. And although it is difficult to imagine, this form of camp entertainment included songs, poems, jokes, and even stand-up comedy (some with underlying satire about the camp) performed by anyone who wanted to. This activity was meaningful in part because it helped the prisoners forget their horrific situation, even if only for a moment. Frankl reported, "Generally speaking, any pursuit of art in camp was somewhat grotesque. But you might be even more astonished to learn that one could find a sense of humor there as well. *Humor was another of the soul's weapons in the fight for self-preservation* [emphasis added]."[80]

In fact, Frankl trained a friend to develop a sense of humor in one of the camps. He suggested to this friend that they promise each other to invent at least one amusing story daily, and it had to be about some incident that could happen after their liberation. One story involved a future dinner engagement, during which Frankl's friend would forget where he was when the soup was served and beg the hostess to ladle it "from the bottom." This request was significant because the camps provided only thin watery soup; servings "from the bottom," which were extremely rare, might include peas and therefore would be a special treat!

It's important to distinguish between self-detachment and denial. When we detach, we do so consciously and with an orientation toward action. We understand our predicament and choose to behave in a way that supports our relationship with others. We might share our burden at work; we might not. But we know what it is and we know what we are doing. In contrast, denial separates us from our experience and the benefits that can be derived from it. And when we deny our own experience, we deny the experience of others. Denial thus leads to disconnection. Self-detachment, on the other hand, leads to connection, learning, and growth.

Developing the Skill of Self-Detachment

Frankl frequently employed the technique of self-detachment during his imprisonment in the concentration camps. Often he kept himself going by imagining himself as an observer rather than as a prisoner. Here's how he disclosed to one conference audience how he had used self-detachment for his own survival:

I repeatedly tried to distance myself from the misery that surrounded me by externalizing it. I remember marching one morning from the camp to the work site, hardly able to bear the hunger, the cold, and the pain of my frozen and festering feet, so swollen from hunger edema and squeezed into my shoes. My situation seemed bleak, even hopeless. Then I imagined that I stood at the lectern in a large, beautiful, warm and bright hall. I was about to give a lecture to an interested audience on "Psychotherapeutic Experiences in a Concentration Camp" (the actual title that he later used at that conference). In the imaginary lecture I reported the things that I am now living through. Believe me, ladies and gentlemen, at that moment I could not dare to hope that some day it would be my good fortune to actually give such a lecture.[81]

Being able to use your imagination effectively to visualize directly supports and influences the self-detachment principle. Experience has also shown that self-detachment can be facilitated by immersing yourself in a role (much like an actor) other than yourself. Hence, a useful exercise for practicing self-detachment is creating a part for yourself in either the movie of your own life or in some other movie production in which you must perform a key role.

For example, imagine that you are the principal character in the movie *Defending Your Life*. In Judgment City, they showed video clips of your life's moments of greatest fear. If you were in Judgment City, what fears would you be confronting and how would you deal with them? How would you justify or defend your actions in the past? Your sense of responsibility for discovering personal meaning can be heightened by immersing yourself in such a fictional, yet still autobiographical, detached view of your own life.

Of course, in the final analysis, self-detachment is not about detachment at all. And while it has proved to be an effective tool for coping with a wide range of stressful situations, including predicaments and hardships from which escape is impossible, its ultimate value lies in its unlimited potential for bringing wholeness and authentic meaning to life. To summon the power of self-detachment and tap into this potential requires both freedom of thought and a will to meaning. And we can only fulfill these requirements if we are not prisoners of our thoughts.

Meaning Moment Recall a situation in your personal life or work life from which you felt the need to distance yourself before you could find a proper resolution (this may even be your situation today). Perhaps you were faced with a family or business decision that wasn't aligned with your personal values or ethics. Perhaps you were thrust into an emergency situation that required swift action. How did you distance or detach yourself from the situation? How did you distance or detach yourself from yourself, so that you could view and review your own attitudes and behaviors? As you think about the situation now, what did you learn from it? In particular, what did you learn about your capacity for self-detachment? In hindsight, what could you have done differently in this situation?

Meaning Question: How do you use humor as a way of putting distance between yourself and a challenge in your personal life and work, instead of getting obsessed with the situation?

Look at Yourself from a Distance

FOR FURTHER REFLECTION

Think about the ways in which you can help your co-workers learn and practice self-detachment at work — as a coping mechanism and a tool for learning and growth. How would you ask them to demonstrate that they understand and can apply this principle? How could you help your family members or friends to learn and practice self-detachment in their lives to deal with stress and promote learning and growth? How would you ask them to demonstrate that they understand and can apply this principle?

Shift Your Focus
of Attention

De-reflection can only be attained to the degree to which
. . . awareness is directed toward positive aspects.[82]

Andy is a former executive with a major software company. He used to make more than $130,000 a year and had a terrific benefits package. He supervised teams of software programmers in several states and had an office overseas. But no more. Like scores of other well-paid, white-collar workers, Andy was laid off and has been unable to find a job that offers the same—or even similar—responsibilities, status, salary, and benefits. Instead, out of desperation, he has found himself grasping at survival jobs offering considerably less.

"Yes, desperate times require desperate measures," says Andy. He continues, "This is no time to be picky. Since they laid me off, I've sold jewelry in a department store and worked as a cashier at a ski slope, both at eight dollars an hour. Now I sell golf equipment."

Andy, however, is more than a mere survivor in a job

market that calls for such desperate measures. Although he is empathetic, Andy doesn't really see himself as grasping at straws like some displaced white-collar workers. He would say that he's not in the same boat at all. You see, Andy isn't driven by frustration, money worries, shame, or embarrassment. In fact, Andy doesn't feel that he is going backward; instead, he feels that he's going forward. An avid golfer, he has moved on to jobs related to his hobby—first helping run the pro shop at a local golf course and now selling golf equipment in a mall sports shop. And in his current job, Andy sees an even more positive side.

"It's a lot simpler and less challenging than it used to be, but I've learned to be humble," he says. "I see guys coming on to the golf course wound pretty tight. They're guys who come in and are late for their tee times and they expect me to do something. I enjoy dealing with people who remind me what I *used* to be like."

Andy has learned a great deal since he was cut from his executive job. He has been able to see the silver lining in what could have been a cloud of despair and a time of inner emptiness. Instead, Andy has shifted his focus to more important matters in his life and has discovered deeper personal meaning in the process.

> Other things being equal, an unemployed person who maintains his morale will have better chances in the competitive struggle than a person who has become apathetic. He will, for example, be more likely to get a job which both apply for.[83]

Throughout my own childhood, whenever things went wrong, a voice from inside my head said, "Think about something else." And I would. I remember once, when I was a teenager, during a jumping competition I was thrown into a water jump and the horse fell on top of me. As I lay submerged in the water, I thought about whether my horse was alright, whether we would still complete the course, and whether I'd get my homework assignment completed in time for school on Monday morning. I even remember asking myself questions, such as what was my name, assuring myself that I was still alive if I could answer correctly!

As kids, we are naturally resilient; nothing keeps us down for long. Our attention spans are short, our interests many, and our involvement with whatever is happening is complete. Most of us knew instinctively how to "think of something else" should someone hurt our feelings, steal our toys, or eat our candy. We might yell and scream for a few moments, but not for long. It wasn't natural to hold onto our thoughts, to become obsessed about wrongdoings. We'd simply get on to the next big adventure. There was always something more exciting to think about and do.

When we're grown up this skill is shelved. As adults we learn to think things through, which is useful. But when thinking becomes obsession and we dwell repeatedly upon negative things, it's not so useful anymore. Often our work, at which we spend such a large part of our lives, becomes the scapegoat for obsessive complaining and negativity. Things are unfair; the boss is a jerk; the co-workers don't cooperate; lunch is too short; the day is too long; the work is too much; the pay is not enough. Sometimes it seems that work exists simply to give us something to complain about.

Shifting from Complaining

We have all complained, and we all know complainers. Some-times we like them because they do our complaining for us and allow us to vent our frustrations without risk. Other times com-plainers weigh us down with their misery, and we can feel our own mood and energy taking a dive. When we become locked into our own complaining shadow and focus on all the bad stuff, we immediately lose sight of the good stuff. Blaming and complaining get us nowhere, even if we face real problems. It's time to dust off those old childhood skills, think about some-thing else, and get on with life.

Years ago, I was working in Illinois for the state depart-ment of mental health. I was responsible for coordinating social services within a subregion of the city of Chicago and was working with an inpatient psychiatric unit in one of the state's mental health facilities.

This particular facility, along with others in the metro-politan Chicago area, was overcrowded with patients, many of whom were either psychotic or prone to violence, and my unit was suffering from a severe shortage of staff. For these and other reasons, both union and nonunion employees complained incessantly about the problems we were facing. Patients, we knew, had a right to the most humane treatment possible, and we weren't doing a very good job of provid-ing it. In fact, I would say that we were doing a horrible job because we found it almost impossible to meet even the most basic standards of care. The facility was so overcrowded that patients were sleeping on the floor in the hallways! In short, we weren't even meeting our ethical and moral obligations to care properly for our fellow human beings.

Well, the complaining by staff continued, and an increasing number of employees came down with the "blue flu," which meant that they called in sick and made an already bad staffing situation worse. Those of us in supervisory or management positions staffed the agency as well as we could, frequently working multiple eight-hour shifts. Eventually, the complaining and resistance escalated into a full-blown walk-out and strike led by union officials.

I remember my boss, Rita, a registered nurse and long-time mental health administrator, saying, "Good for them! However, the show has to go on, so let's see what we can do without them."

"Without them?" I thought. "How are we going to do that? We're in a serious predicament with no obvious resolution. Maybe she just doesn't get it."

As I now know, that was not the case. Rita knew much more than I gave her credit for. For one thing, she focused on the potentially *positive* implications of the walkout—that we might finally get the resources we had needed for so long. Second, she stressed how much camaraderie was being discovered among those who were left minding the psychiatric unit. We were getting to know each other better and were relying on each other more than ever. For Rita, our situation was reminiscent of her medical MASH-type unit in Vietnam. She had survived that situation, and she was damn sure she would do the same this time around. Rita saw that the patients themselves (some of them anyway) had the capacity to help *us* out in our time of need. And we did find support among the patient ranks, and working together bonded us in ways that traditional modes of therapy could never have done.

Shift Your Focus of Attention

By shifting our focus to positive experiences, we were able to find the potential for meaning in our predicament. Inspired by Rita's guidance and capacity to de-reflect, as Frankl would say, we were not subdued by our circumstances no matter how dire they appeared to be. Thanks, Rita.

Creative Distraction

Two things happen when we think good thoughts on the job: we feel better at work and we are better at working. If we use creative distraction when we are upset and frustrated, we see ourselves more fully, more generously. We move out from under our own shadow and open ourselves to constructive action.

When we are in a miserable job situation, our choices are to either quit or find meaning in what we are doing. Remember, unless you have an armed Nazi guard dictating your every move, you still have the freedom to choose whether to leave or stay in your job. This said, finding meaning sometimes means distracting ourselves from what we don't like, because even when we do love our jobs, we all experience bad, even ugly, days.

When we are stressed at work, we can always conjure something else: a favorite place, a favorite activity, even a favorite smell. One person I know decorates her office with mementos from trips she has taken around the world. When work grows stressful, she focuses on a favorite vacation spot and, in *Star Trek* fashion, transports herself to it until she relaxes. Another person imagines himself sailing, often using aromatherapy and music to help shift him into the spirit of his vision. Your image of escape could be anything: use whatever works—it's *your* imagination.

Italian film producer and actor Roberto Benigni is known for using his imagination in ways that allow his audiences to take mental excursions without traveling anywhere. In his internationally acclaimed, Academy-Award–winning movie, *Life Is Beautiful*, Benigni shares his sentimental tale about a man trying to shield his son from the horrors of the Holocaust. The movie has been criticized by those who feel it unrealistically and inappropriately makes light of and pokes fun at events that were so horrific, but Benigni's "comedy" was based on the ungainly story of his father's two-year ordeal in a Nazi labor camp and therefore is grounded in reality.

The film tells the story of Guido, a Jewish waiter who, while imprisoned in a camp, creates and plays an imaginative game (you'll have to see the movie to discover the rules of this game) with his young son to avoid breaking down and giving up. To avoid seeing his son killed at the hands of the Nazis or demoralized by the horror of the situation, Guido (played by Benigni himself) keeps up his rapid-fire humor and lighthearted, positive outlook in the face of everything.

It has been said, "Don't sweat the small stuff. And it's all small stuff."[84] This advice is especially true at work. No matter how important we are in the company or organization, in the grand scheme of things, it's small stuff that makes up our jobs. Most of the time, someone else could do our jobs, which doesn't make them, or us, less meaningful. It means that we should always pay attention to our freedom of imagination—to play, hike, cook, write science fiction, become president of a small country—which is always available to us. To quote Albert Einstein, "Imagination is more important than knowledge."

With our habit of turning to television, video games, and the Web, we often forget that we have access to our imagination at any moment. We have almost trained ourselves out of imagining. But if you talk with anyone who has survived trauma or has overcome hardship, they usually say that their imagination is their best friend.

In the concentration camps, as Roberto Benigni's Guido did, Frankl seized on various fantasies to fight off despair. He envisioned meeting his mother once more and visiting with his wife. He imagined himself climbing mountains again—one of his favorite pastimes. And he fantasized about personal pleasures, such as having a warm bath, and more public ones, such as lecturing to a packed auditorium. In the latter image, he said, his own ambition helped prevent final despondency.

For prisoners, it's often food that stimulates their imaginations and sends them off on mental journeys. They recreate, over and over, the meal they will eat when they are free. In imagination they create the colors, textures, tastes, and scents of this food so vividly that the meal sees them through years of isolation and hopelessness. It's a meal that offers meaning to their lives.

When we become too focused on what's in front of us at work—whether it's an oppressive manager, a wayward employee, a complicated task, or a boring routine—it's like looking at the earth from space and focusing on just one rain cloud over Idaho. We need to remember that life is huge, and so are our lives. When we grow distressed about our jobs and work, we lose sight of the meaning in our lives. Our ability to detach from the distress and focus imaginatively on something that pleases us can return us to our freedom and to our source of authentic meaning.

Creative distraction, or de-reflection, to use Frankl's word, is also useful when we have to do something really important at work, such as give a presentation or participate in a crucial meeting. By paying attention to our breathing and to tension in our bodies, and by imagining ourselves in a safe, nurturing place, we can calm ourselves. We can return to our selves, and not be so vulnerable to whatever role we think we are expected to play. When we bring our authentic, centered selves to the situation, even if we don't always know the right thing to say, we speak from our inherent author-ity, the person we are. This is something to which we are all sensitive. We all recognize when someone is being authentic, and we feel comfortable: we like them and feel at ease. By drawing imaginatively from the source of our authenticity, we can move beyond role playing in our jobs. An ethics of authenticity emerges, and real work can begin.[85]

We may believe that we must maintain our roles because they are what people expect. To do so, we do and say what most enhances our vision of our role at work. But in the long run, such an effort is exhausting—for us and for others. It is important to remember that knowing our job and playing a role are two different things. Giving up the role-playing to be who we are and doing our job is the most powerful combina-tion of all.

Sometimes we need help to shift from role-playing to authenticity, and it is our ability to de-reflect creatively that can help us the most. It is always available. Just imagine.

Often when we de-reflect—that is, shift our focus of

attention—from what is bothering us at work (or in our personal life), we gain insight into the problem. For instance, many of our challenges with others stem from the fact that the ways we see things, make decisions, and do our jobs differs from those of someone we work with. Such differences can seem huge. How we perceive these differences can get a big boost from a little de-reflection, leading to constructive resolutions.

> De-reflection is intended to counteract . . . compulsive inclination to self-observation.[86]

The principle of de-reflection, Frankl would say, helps us to ignore those aspects of our life and work that should be ignored. It also helps to lead us from absorption in our problems toward the true meanings that await our discovery. In effect, de-reflection encourages us to perceive something new in a situation so that we are able let go of our old perceptions and patterns of behavior. Through this meaning-centered process, we are able to mature by transcending those conditions that limit us, so that we can make new commitments and identify those things that can (and should) be avoided.

Practicing De-reflection

A simple exercise can help you practice de-reflection and deal with real, practical issues at work and in your everyday life. It's called the Mental Excursion Exercise. In addition to helping you shift your focus of attention and take a mental journey elsewhere, this exercise can be used to facilitate creative thinking and problem solving.

Begin by jotting on a piece of paper the situation, problem, or predicament you are facing. Now list situations that are similar to yours, making sure that you stretch your imagination as much as possible by deferring judgment. Enjoy the process of free association and making connections in your mind. Remember, you are trying to escape from your problem situation, so identify situations that are different from each other. As a catalyst and guide, fill in the blanks of the following sentence: "My problem situation, [What is it?], is like [What is analogous to my situation?]." For example, "The challenge of having to merge two different organizations is like getting married." Once again, stretch your thinking!

Now select at least two analogous problem situations from your list and brainstorm what you would need to do or have to resolve each of these situations. In the sample analogy, for example, what might you need to do in the process of getting married? Record your thoughts in a list, without pausing to edit, trying to capture as many ideas as possible.

Congratulations! You've taken a mental excursion—actually, two or more excursions. Now return to your original issue—your point of departure, so to speak—and spend some time generating ideas for possible solutions to it. The best way to do this step is to make connections with the items you listed as necessary to resolve the analogous problem situations. Since you chose situations that were similar to your original one, you know right away that there is a relationship between the situations. Your mission is to use your lists of items to resolve the analogous problem situations (for example, the things you identified that need to be done in the process of getting married) as a springboard for generating ideas that might be used to approach, or even resolve, your original problem situation (for example, merging two different organizations). Two ideas that might come to mind are (1) decide where to live (office location) and how to merge two households (offices), and (2) invite the families (executive teams) to a rehearsal party.

We all bring different histories, experiences, skills, and motivations to our jobs. When we incorporate a bit of de-reflection into our processes, we invite others to be as effective as they know how to be without anyone feeling judged by the differences.

Exercising our ability to de-reflect difficulties at work helps us to be more resilient. We may even feel more confident because we have a reliable, constructive way of coping when situations become difficult. This mindset can serve us in minor challenges, such as deciding what kind of office equipment to buy, and in big ones, such as how to deal with losing our jobs.

In a perfect world, the jobs we love would be ours forever. But more and more skilled people are faced with losing their jobs after many years of employment. Sometimes the job loss is a sudden shock—we are forced into action with no warning. At other times we can see it coming—the possibility, if not always the probability. In either case, fear and anxiety accompany the insecurity. The situation and our emotions can make us gear up to be better and more productive employees, or we can shift our focus from our immediate investment in our job and imaginatively look up and out over our personal horizons. The possibilities are unlimited, and the choice is ours.

Our ability to forget ourselves and focus our attention

can be very useful in the search for meaning in both our personal lives and our work lives. When it helps us reconnect to who we are, who we love, and what's worth doing, de-reflection restores us above and beyond our jobs and our money. No longer prisoners of our thoughts, we are restored to an awareness of meaning.

 Meaning Moment Recall a situation in your personal or work life from which you felt the need to shift your attention to deal with it effectively (this may even be your situation today). Perhaps you were faced with a family or business problem that was especially stressful. Maybe you were thrust into an emergency that required swift action. How did you shift your focus from the situation to something else? What did you imagine or fantasize about? What, if anything, did you do as a result of your shift of focus? As you think about the situation now, what did you learn from it? In particular, what did you learn about your capacity for de-reflection? In hindsight, what could you have done differently in this situation?

 Meaning Question: In what ways do you use your imagination to refocus your attention when dealing with problematic situations in your personal life and at work?

FOR FURTHER REFLECTION

Think about the ways in which you can help your co-workers learn and practice de-reflection at work — as a coping mechanism and a tool for learning and growth. How would you ask them to demonstrate that they understand and can apply this principle? Now think about the ways in which you can help your family members or friends learn and practice de-reflection in their lives — as a coping mechanism and a tool for learning and growth. What would you ask them to do to demonstrate that they understand and can apply this principle?

Extend
Beyond
Yourself

Don't aim at success — the more you aim at it and make it a target, the more you are going to miss it. For success, like happiness, cannot be pursued; it must ensue and it only does so as the unintended side-effect of one's dedication to a cause greater than oneself or as the by-product of one's surrender to a person other than oneself. Happiness must happen, and the same holds for success: you have to let it happen by not caring about it.[87]

Andrea Jaeger was the youngest seeded player in Wimbledon history in 1980. At only fifteen years old, she was also the youngest U.S. Open semifinalist that same year. Described as a "pigtailed, teenage wunderkind," Andrea was positioned for continued athletic success and fame. Yet by 1984 her career in tennis had ended because of injuries and burnout, and Andrea disappeared from the sports radar screen and the public's eye.

Andrea Jaeger's life had taken a turn, but her legacy was just beginning to unfold. During her years as a tennis phenomenon, Andrea had spent her time off with sick children in hospitals around the world. Through these heartfelt encounters, Andrea's true metamorphosis was taking place.

After moving to Aspen, Colorado, in 1989, she made the decision to dedicate her life to terminally ill children, to give them a greater opportunity to experience life.

"The whole mission was to bring opportunities for children with cancer and other life-threatening diseases to enhance their lives and to make things possible on a long-term basis," Jaeger said.

Jaeger created a charity, the Kids' Stuff Foundation, and with the help of friends and other supporters, brought children from all over the world to Colorado for a week at a time to experience life outside the hospital room. At first Andrea relied on local hotels to accommodate her young visitors. However, with the development of the ten-acre Silver Lining Ranch, built totally through donations, Andrea's dream for a properly designed facility became a reality. In June 1999 the first children, twenty in all, arrived to stay at the ranch, and Andrea was there to greet them.

The Silver Lining Ranch, which is within the Aspen city limits, touches every soul in addition to attending to the children's individual needs. Groups are kept small intentionally: "I believe in the philosophy of one child at a time," Jaeger says. She continues: "If you can make a child smile or laugh, well, your place in the world has been preserved. You carry a lot of what the kids bring, and when you see the strength, the character, the hope in their eyes and hearts, it gets you through the darkest hours you could ever have fund-raising."

In July 2001 Andrea Jaeger was interviewed on NBC Dateline. After a tour of the ranch, the interviewer was so impressed she asked Jaeger, "How do you want to be remembered?" Without having to think, Jaeger quickly replied, "I don't need to be remembered. I want the *kids* to be remembered." In no small way, Andrea's response shows us that the heart's light within the human spirit is most brightly illuminated when we create meaning beyond our own lives.

When we work creatively and productively with others, our experience of meaning can be profound. When we work directly for the good of others, meaning deepens in ways that reward us beyond measure. Whenever we go beyond satisfying our own personal needs, we enter the realm of what Frankl called ultimate meaning. Other people call it connection to a higher self, to God, to our own spirit, to universal consciousness, to love, to the collective good. Frankl's decision to call his unique approach to psychotherapy Logotherapy is significant in a spiritual sense too. Besides being roughly translated as "the meaning," the root word, *logos*, a common Greek word, also has deep spiritual meaning and implications. No matter what it's called, ultimate meaning is deep meaning, and it transforms our lives.

The Spirit of Play at Work

We all recognize team spirit when we feel it, but what exactly is it? A leading authority on team spirit offered the following observation:

> *When you ask people . . . what it is like being part of a great team, what is most striking is the meaningfulness of the experience. People talk about being part of something larger than themselves, of being connected, of being generative. It becomes quite clear that, for many, their experiences as part of truly great teams stand out as singular periods of life lived to the fullest. Some spend the rest of their lives looking for ways to recapture that spirit.*[88]

Team spirit is bigger than we are— no matter how large our group is—yet it cannot exist without us. And no matter what our goal is, team spirit itself is not goal oriented. Rather, team spirit grows out of doing and being together. It is part of the process. The results, or product, always come later.

On the playing field, whether in sports or in business, team spirit raises everybody's individual spirits. When team spirit is alive, anything becomes possible. And even when the result is a smashing success, the personal rewards are always more profound *during* the process. What we remember as deeply meaningful and transformative is the being and doing together—the playing.

What sport, theater, and every job on the planet have in common is the potential for play. When we give and take, when we are there for one another—on the field and off—it's play that brings us together. Play provides rewards that reach beyond ourselves, anchoring meaning somewhere "out there," where it means something to us all, and beyond us all.

Paradoxically, focusing too much on the goal removes us from play and makes the goal more difficult to reach. And the place where play—this wonderful manifestation of the human condition—is most likely to be squelched is where it's most needed: at work. Being a boss is often like being a parent: we forget everything we learned along the way about play. We forget about fun and games and how well we learn and grow without being told how. Our natural inclination is toward playing together cooperatively and joyfully. Yet in the workplace many managers go into meltdown. Call in the brigades, work is not being taken seriously! Stop the fun before it spreads! Shoot the bastards!

How many of us have had this experience? We're just getting somewhere with the task at hand or the problem of the day—whether it's as an individual or part of a group—and we get caught having fun. Immediately the creative wind is sucked right out of our sails. Spirits are dampened; the progress we've made is tarnished. It's usually only much later, when enough time has passed to allow us to recreate our feelings of success, that progress is restarted. If only those beleaguered managers knew what a disservice they are doing to the company when they dampen the spirit of creative play at work. It's what creates exuberance and keeps us at our most productive. If we can't freely express creative play, this reward that costs the company nothing is destroyed.

Growing Meaning in a Corporation

Whenever our work takes us outside ourselves, we experience greater meaning, whether it's doing something as simple as choosing a location for the next company retreat or as complex as creating a meaning-based multinational corporation. When we work to bring meaning to a company, beyond the bottom line, we bring meaning to everyone who works there and to life itself. This is a gargantuan task when it comes to the corporate world because the sole task of a corporation, as a legal entity, is to grow money. Growing meaning is not in its job description. But the stockholders, CEOs, and the employees can, if they are heroic, grow meaning in a corporation.

Throughout this book, we've seen examples of excellent companies that are focused on objectives beyond money, where the quest for personal meaning and fulfillment really matters. But what about those companies that espouse such existential values, and yet the rubber never meets the road? I'm not talking about organizations that clearly have no intention of growing meaning but those that say they do.

Years ago, I worked with George, the president and CEO of a mid-sized corporation that specialized in the development of state-of-the-art technologies to promote human potential. Thanks to George's solid reputation in his scientific field from working in the space program, his company was able to recruit some of the best scientists in the country and attract substantial investments of capital. George was flamboyant and charismatic, and he loved being in the media spotlight (where he found himself often).

As both a leader and manager, George presented himself as a sort of guru, having self-published a book that laid out his philosophy of life and business. George saw everyone as interconnected, professing that the whole was greater than the sum of the parts. Moreover, he said that his company was intentionally designed and managed on such principles, presumably to ensure that meaning at work, and meaningful work, would always play a central role in his company. But even though George talked the talk and hugged all of his employees—including frequent group hugs—I observed low morale, high turnover, distrust, and disrespect throughout the company's ranks. Good intentions aren't enough to grow anything, let alone meaning.

Living Beyond Ourselves

We all know individuals who live beyond themselves and for others in their work lives and personal lives. Usually, they seem to be doing it because it's in their nature or because they have been blessed with good mentors along their path—including parents, teachers, and bosses, who have guided them by example. I suspect, moreover, that their giving natures often grow out of personal experience. Perhaps they suffered as kids and know what it's like, so they became foster parents. Perhaps they were raised with a lot of money and comfort in their lives and want to give back, so they joined the Peace Corps. Maybe they rose to the top of their profession, found it wanting, searched for deeper meaning, and then got a job in a low-paying, nonprofit organization that serves others. Perhaps they've been to the top of their profession, loved it, and been inspired to help others.

If we take a few minutes to look around in our lives, every day we will see people doing things for others, quietly, unexpectedly, and without compensation. If we were to ask why, they might not have ready answers. But I suspect they would all agree that it feels good. Selflessness feels good. It satisfies something in us that yearns to transcend ourselves, that knows we are honoring a deeper meaning in life when we serve the needs of others.

The capacity to extend beyond yourself, according to Frankl, is another one of our unique traits as human beings. Indeed, *self-transcendence*, as it is referred to in Logotherapy, is the essence of our humanness. Put differently, being human basically means focusing on and relating to something other than oneself. Recognizing the abstract nature of self-transcendence, Frankl uses the human eye as an analogy:

> *In a way, your eyes are self-transcendent as well. Just notice that the capacity of the eye to perceive the surrounding world is ironically dependent on its incapacity to perceive itself, except in a mirror. At the moment my eye perceives something of itself, for instance a halo with colors around a light, it perceives its own glaucoma. At the moment I see clouding I perceive my own cataract, something of my own eye. But the healthy eye, the normal*

*eye, doesn't see anything of itself. The seeing capacity is impaired
to the very extent to which the eye perceives something of itself.[89]*

Although such a comparison with the healthy eye helps
us better understand the nature of self-transcendence, another transformational quality may help us come to terms with
why self-transcendence is so vitally important. A humanistic concept advanced in South Africa, called Ubuntu,[90] not
only provides the foundation for African management but
also is pertinent to our understanding of self-transcendence.
The full expression in Zulu of this concept is *ubuntu ngumuntu ngabantu*, translated roughly into English as "a person is
only a person through other persons." Ubuntu is not about
relationships per se; rather, it is about the way human beings
establish their own humanness by recognizing and reaching
out to the humanness of others. I propose that it is because of
Ubuntu—that is, because humanness can only be expressed
by caring for others—that self-transcendence occurs. In
effect, we must be able to extend beyond ourselves so that we
can fulfill or realize more of ourselves.

To gain an appreciation for the reflective basis for self-transcendence, let me share with you the following story,
called "The Echo":[91]

> A son and his father are walking in the mountains. Suddenly, the
> son falls, hurts himself, and screams: "AAAhhhhhhhhhhh!!!"
> To his surprise, he hears a voice repeating, somewhere in the
> mountains: "AAAhhhhhhhhhhh!!!" Curious, he yells out: "Who
> are you?" He receives the answer: "Who are you?" And then he
> screams to the mountain: "I admire you!" The voice answers: "I
> admire you!" Angered at the response, he screams: "Coward!"
> He receives the answer: "Coward!" He looks to his father and
> asks: "What's going on?" The father smiles and says: "My son,
> pay attention." Again, the boy screams: "You are a champion!"

The voice answers: "You are a champion!" The boy is surprised, but does not understand. Then the father explains: "People call this Echo, but really this is Life. It gives you back everything you say or do." Our life is simply a reflection of our actions. If you want more love in the world, create more love in your heart. If you want more competence in your team, improve your own competence. This relationship applies to everything, in all aspects of life. Life will give you back everything you have given to it. Your life is not a coincidence. It's a reflection of you!

Now stop and think for a moment. Are you paying attention and listening to your echo? From what life seems to be calling out to you, what are you calling out to life?

Miracle on the Hudson

It is called the "miracle on the Hudson." On Thursday, January 15, 2009, US Airways flight 1549 crashed into the Hudson River minutes after takeoff from New York City's LaGuardia Airport. After being crippled by a collision with a flock of birds, the plane carrying 155 passengers went down just feet from the Manhattan skyline. Miraculously, all passengers and crew members survived.

While commercial jet crashes fortunately are rare, surviving a major airline accident such as that of US Airways flight 1549 is even rarer. Luck and good fortune were obviously at work in this particular case. So was the unquestioned expertise of the pilot, Chesley B. "Sully" Sullenberger, who became a national hero, copilot Jeffrey Skiles, and their crew for the way they handled the abrupt and unusual landing and evacuation. Expertise was also displayed by the crews of the U.S. Coast Guard vessels, tour boats, and commuter ferries who quickly came to the plane's rescue.

This was an unforgettable life-and-death experience. And the level of expertise and professional readiness of everyone involved in the entire rescue effort cannot be overlooked or minimized. This said, the real-life drama of and lessons learned from US Airways flight 1549 go well beyond strict professionalism and first responder experience per se. The actions that began with Captain Sullenberger and his crew, and that continued with everyone, including passengers, who played a part in ensuring that all people safely departed the plane and were rescued, underscore that something else was at work too. And although this something else might be viewed as part of the "miracle" that unfolded on the Hudson, I submit that it is also a manifestation of something more practical and realistic: the elevation of the human spirit at work in the service of others, or self-transcendence—that is, extending beyond oneself.

Think about it for a minute. A potential catastrophe with loss of human life was averted on the Hudson River by the actions of people caring for and helping other people in need, even at the risk of their own safety and welfare. Over and over again, from the stories of US Airways flight 1549, we heard about civility and heroism that went well beyond the call of duty.

As the aircraft began to sink into the Hudson River's frigid gray current, witnesses described a scene of level-headed teamwork to evacuate the weak and injured, including an infant and an elderly woman in a wheelchair. Moreover, as passengers scrambled for the exits, they did so in as calm a way as possible under the circumstances, even carrying the helpless and ignoring their own fear so that everyone filed quickly and safely through the exit doors and out onto the wings and the emergency chutes. All of this was accomplished under extremely harsh conditions — most passengers were not properly dressed for being outdoors and they fled without their life jackets. A few even fell into the 36-degree water, where hypothermia would have quickly taken their lives.

However, fellow passengers, who effectively were strangers, displayed unselfish acts of courage, risking their lives to fish their fallen comrades out of the water! And I'm not yet talking about the bravery exhibited by the plane's pilot and crew or the first responders and other emergency personnel who came to the aid of the stranded passengers! No, once again, I'm talking about ordinary people helping other ordinary people under circumstances that simply boggle the mind. For example, I read about one passenger, who, although soaked and shivering from having been in the river, turned her attention to a fellow passenger who had suffered a deep gash in her leg and was bleeding heavily. Despite the obvious propensity for chaos all around her, this truly volunteer aid worker observed that the most amazing thing was that she saw no pushing or shoving — only help and compassion. How is this for a practical example of the spirit of service and the Echo?

There is no question that the rescue of US Airways flight 1549 inspired millions of people around the world. Moreover, as I have already pointed out, there was no shortage of heroes on the Hudson that day. Captain Sullenberger, a former fighter pilot, went up and down the listing, drifting craft — twice — to make sure that everyone got out before he did the same. And

those aboard the Coast Guard vessels, tour boats, and commuter ferries worked hard and fast to rescue the people from
the jetliner, even giving them their gloves, jackets, and coats
to prevent hypothermia. A couple of New York City police
detectives selflessly entered the plane to rescue some passengers who were still inside, while their police scuba diver colleagues dropped from a helicopter high above to pull some
passengers from the icy water. If the accident itself was hard
to imagine, so was the result: except for one person with two
broken legs, there were no other reports of serious injuries, and
all 155 people on board were pulled to safety.

Yes, be realistic and expect miracles, I say! By directing attention to something beyond ourselves, it is possible
(and realistic) to manifest the human spirit at work and turn
what could be meaningless suffering into a genuine human
achievement. This is what occurred on the Hudson River
on January 15, 2009, when human beings demonstrated that
they can—and will—rise above their predicament, against
the odds, and manifest the spirit of service by extending
beyond themselves. Moreover, I'm sure that everyone associated with the "miracle on the Hudson," even those who only
observed it from afar, discovered deep personal meaning in
the experience.

The Path of Forgiveness

The yearning to be of deep service often grows out of deep
suffering. Viktor Frankl, Nelson Mandela, Mahatma Gandhi,
the Dalai Lama, Archbishop Desmond Tutu, Aung San Suu
Kyi—all transformed their suffering into service. They experienced their suffering as meaningful in the most profound

ways. It wasn't bitterness that resulted from their suffering, it was love—and *meaning*. The sacredness of being human was the legacy of their suffering and it informed and transformed the rest of their lives. Meaning became their life's work.

We aren't all called to be a Mandela or a Gandhi. But if we pay attention, we will find that life calls to us every day to go beyond our own interests. And when we do, our own interests are served in ways that are inexplicably and profoundly meaningful.

Perhaps the most challenging thing we can do to go beyond ourselves is to forgive. At work, this is especially hard because our emotional ties may not be as strong, and therefore neither is the motivation to forgive. Yet when we look at forgiveness in the light of others' ability to forgive, the path should not seem so daunting.

Frankl didn't subscribe to the concept of collective guilt, and whenever possible he fought this idea, even though it was an unpopular stand after the war. He also forgave his Nazi guards; he even felt compassion for them. In *Man's Search for Meaning*, he tells about the SS officer who was the head of the concentration camp from which Frankl was finally liberated. After his liberation, Frankl learned that this SS man "had secretly spent considerable sums of his own money at the drugstore in the nearby village, purchasing medications for the camp inmates."[92]

Nelson Mandela walked a path of forgiveness during and after his nearly thirty years of imprisonment. It almost seems as though meaning holds forgiveness at its core—that we can't reach life's deeper meaning without going through forgiveness of ourselves and others.

Forgiveness means letting go of our suffering. It has much more to do with our own well-being than with that of the person we forgive. When we hold on to our suffering—our resentment, hurt, and anger—we are inside ourselves with self-pity. Our suffering becomes a veil through which we see ourselves and others, something we have to feed, keep alive, and justify. If we don't, we believe we allow the other person to be "right" in their unjust treatment of us.

But forgiveness does not mean forgetting, diminishing, or condoning the misdeed. It has much more to do with free-ing ourselves from its hold. In fact, forgiving can be one of the most powerful things we do. Our ability to live our lives with love and generosity—impeded when we hold on to our grievances—is freed when we forgive. We don't have to love or be generous to the woman who was disloyal to us at work or the man who belittled our ideas at a staff meeting, but when we forgive them, we liberate ourselves from captivity. Love and generosity will return in their own time.

The search for meaning in our lives takes us on paths large and small. When we go beyond ourselves—whether in service, forgiveness, unselfishness, thoughtfulness, gener-osity, and understanding toward others—we enter into the spiritual realm of meaning. By giving beyond ourselves, we make our own lives richer. This long-understood truth is at the heart of all meaningful spiritual traditions. It's a mystery that can only be experienced. And when we do experience it, we are in the heart of meaning. We are no longer prisoners of our thoughts.

Meaning Moment Recall a situation in your personal or work life in which you felt the need to self-transcend, or extend beyond yourself, to deal effectively with it (this may even be your situation today). Perhaps you were faced with a pressing family issue or perplexing customer issue that required an extraordinary response. Maybe you were faced with a question of corporate social responsibility or parental guidance that required some soul-searching for an answer. How did you extend beyond yourself to deal with the situation? What, if anything, did you do as a result of your shift in consciousness? As you think about the situation now, what did you learn from it? In particular, what did you learn about your capacity for self-transcendence? In hindsight, what could you have done differently in this situation?

 Meaning Question: In what ways do you relate and direct to something other than yourself in your life and work?

FOR FURTHER REFLECTION

Think about the ways in which you can help your co-workers learn and practice self-transcendence at work. How could you ask them to demonstrate that they understand and can apply this principle? Think also about the ways in which you can help your family members or friends learn and practice self-transcendence in their lives. What would you ask them to do to demonstrate that they understand and can apply this principle?

Extend Beyond Yourself

Living and Working
with Meaning

*Man's search for meaning is the primary motivation in his life
and not a "secondary rationalization" of instinctual drives.*[93]

"I don't like working with maggots," Rick said to me as we
were discussing his current job and career aspirations. Believe
it or not, Rick was referring to the clients he has as a probation officer for the state department of corrections! He had
worked in his current position for over four years and said
he had not changed his views about the people with whom
he was in daily contact—people who obviously depended on
him for advice and support.

After some probing, I learned that Rick had grown up as
a ward of the state, bouncing between various sets of foster parents, with periodic stints in an orphanage. But rather than making him sympathetic and compassionate toward those in need,
Rick's experience resulted in just the opposite outcome—he
became insensitive and unforgiving. Unlike many people who
have gone through similar situations, Rick couldn't (and didn't

want to) relate to people who in his view weren't able to take care of themselves, who "slurped at the public trough"—that is, who depended on public assistance in some form.

After graduation from college with a degree in finance, Rick took the first full-time job that was available. "Anything would be better than busing tables or flipping burgers," he thought. And although he had never imagined working either in a government or social services position, he jumped at the chance to be a probation officer. Because he needed the full-time work experience, and because he figured he would find something better soon, Rick the probation officer and human services warrior came into being.

Right off the bat he knew this kind of job was not for him, yet he felt trapped. Working full-time for a regular salary was new to him and he liked it—the regular salary, that is. Plus, the state provided a decent benefits package. Most of his friends envied him, and Rick soon found himself working on cruise control. He didn't need to feel; he only needed to put in the hours necessary to receive his paycheck and benefits.

When I talked with Rick, he said that he was feeling more depressed than usual and was having a difficult time getting up in the morning to go to work. During the work day, he said, he felt extremely edgy, he complained a lot (about work, his co-workers, his clients), and he even looked for things to argue about with his supervisor. He was "cruisin' for a bruisin'" and he knew it. He just didn't know what to do about it. He felt lost, confined, unhappy, and unfulfilled.

Whatever we might say about Rick's psychological makeup, I think that we can all agree with this: Rick was in the wrong job! And, more importantly, Rick had become a prisoner of his thoughts. If only he could have recognized that he, and nobody else, held the keys to his own freedom, he could have escaped.

Unlocking Personal Meaning

The keys to unlocking personal meaning in life and at work are, and always have been, within our reach. They are as close as this very moment. Whenever we stop long enough to connect to ourselves, to our environment, to those with whom we live and work, to the task before us, to the extraordinary interdependence that is always part of our lives, we experience meaning. Meaning comes with being who we are in this world. And it is the world that graces us with meaning.

Sometimes we are graced through our very gracelessness. This too can lead us to meaning, perhaps when we least expect it, maybe through chaos and confusion. In our working life we might lay tracks that veer off in one direction just as the train of our life decides to go in a completely different direction. At those times we are a wreck waiting to happen.

Most of us have such times in our lives. The pressures pile on and we adjust and maneuver accordingly. We shift our attitudes, we push our bodies; we reframe our experiences to fit the challenges in our lives. Then something happens and it all falls apart.

When we embrace new possibilities for ourselves, even if they are difficult and challenging, we embrace possibilities for others. And the results can have unanticipated rewards. Viktor Frankl says, "Each of us has his own inner concentration camp...we must deal with, with forgiveness and patience as full human beings; as we are and what we will become."[94]

Living and Working with Meaning

Life has a way of leading us to meaning—if we let it. If we can roll with life's punches and allow ourselves to be humbled by life's blows, we can know deeper and deeper unconditional love for ourselves and others. Or we can toughen up and harden, becoming more resistant and less and less able to love.

There is a saying, "If you want things to stay the same, then something is going to have to change." If there's one thing that does stay the same, it's change. In fact our lives and the world seem to change more and more rapidly and dramatically, offering more opportunities and possibilities, making our choices more complex. We are continually challenged to know who we are, what our values are, and how best to live by them. When we take the time to know ourselves, to know and honor our own integrity, we move deeper into meaning. When we act from the center of who we are and what we represent—honesty, fairness, kindness, and love—our lives are in partnership with meaning, on the job and off. To know we are blessed with meaning, that it graces every aspect and every moment of our lives, is true freedom. At work, it frees us from the judgment of our bosses and co-workers; it frees us to be in tune with what we know best—our own melody of life. It's a melody that only we can sing.

> *The struggle for existence is a struggle "for" something; it is purposeful, and only in so being is it meaningful and able to bring meaning into life.*[95]

When we live and work with meaning, we can choose to see meaning, to cultivate meaning, and to share meaning. We can choose our attitudes to life and work; we can choose how to respond to others, how to respond to our jobs, and how to make the best of difficult circumstances. We can transcend ourselves and be transformed by meaning.

As we awaken to life's meaning inside us, we find that meaning is full of surprises, defying our expectations. We find connections to meaning in the most unusual places and with the most unexpected people, in our personal lives and at work. Our awareness grows, and we become more intensely ourselves and more deeply human.

We will also find that meaning itself changes. What makes sense for us at one time in our working and nonworking lives might not make sense at another time. But when we are rooted in meaning, we can sway much more flexibly, whether it is in a breeze or a hurricane.

Our work lives serve us in unique and meaningful ways that only we truly understand and appreciate. Our work represents our many facets, but it is we who bring light to the work. If our work is fulfilling in and of itself, we know why. If our work serves us beyond the workplace, we know why. It is this knowing why that represents meaning. And knowing why means that we know ourselves and what is calling to us at work—whether it's providing financial responsibility to our loved ones, honoring our unique talents, fulfilling the needs of our families, responding to the needs of the world, being available to do the job that fate sends our way, or any combination of the above.

Meaning Analysis

Let's now take a look at our lives from this "knowing why" perspective. As our frame of reference, let's use one of Frankl's methods of meaning analysis. The aim of meaning analysis is

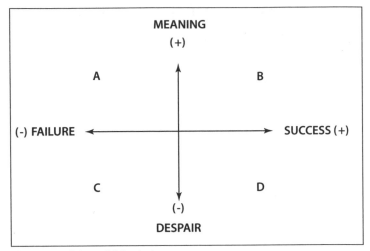

Figure 2. Existential Analysis.

to help people take hold of life by uncovering and focusing on the core values that collectively form the primary motivation in their life: the search for meaning. All human beings, Frankl would say, ultimately have both the freedom and the responsibility to position themselves along two key dimensions of life (see figure 2 above).[96]

The horizontal axis in figure 2 depicts the dimension of *success* (+) and *failure* (−). The vertical axis represents the dimension of *meaning* (+) and *despair* (−), where *meaning* refers to the fulfillment or realization of the person's will to meaning and *despair* is the failure to find meaning or the conviction that life is meaninglessness. Over the course of their lives, people experience different degrees of success in work and their personal lives, and they have a shifting awareness of meaning. They thus find themselves at different points on the graph at different times. In this way the figure can provide a representation of our current existential status.

So how do we use the figure, and what can it tell us? First let's consider how people might be placed in one of the four quadrants or along one of the two axes based on their situation. For example, a wealthy, successful business executive who nevertheless may view his work as unfulfilling or life as devoid of meaning, or both, would be represented by a point somewhere in quadrant D. Think now of other people who might also fall into this category—perhaps someone who is highly successful in a traditional, material sense, yet unfulfilled, suffering from inner emptiness or despair. We all know, or know of, some quadrant D people, don't we? They might be our co-workers, bosses, friends, neighbors, or family members as well as corporate icons, celebrities, or star athletes.

In contrast, consider people who could hardly be considered successful by societal standards—they may exist modestly on a meager salary or pension—but who may be content and happy with their work and everyday life. They might be working in a low-paying, low-profile job or volunteering for a nonprofit cause. In the figure, we would find these people somewhere in quadrant A. Who might you place in this quadrant?

Quadrant B of the figure is the place for people who are *both* successful in a societal sense and fulfilled in a meaning sense. You might recall the story of Tom Chappell and how he effectively moved along the vertical axis toward meaning while remaining on the success side of the horizontal dimension. And don't forget the remarkable, inspirational lives of Christopher and Dana Reeve. Others who exhibit the traits of a quadrant B life can be found in the business world, in sports (let's not forget Andrea Jaeger), in government and politics—indeed, in all sectors of society.

Quadrant C is where we would find those people who could be described as down and out. They are unsuccessful in relative terms and, more importantly, unfulfilled, perhaps even empty, in terms of their sense of personal meaning. Ideally, of course, we'd like to see this particular quadrant empty, but I'm sure you can identify prospective candidates for this quadrant from people you have met.

In essence, this figure is a diagram of life. But what about *your* life? What about *your* work? Where would you place yourself in this two-dimensional space? And where, you should ask yourself, would you *like* to be? In a 1953 letter, Frankl wrote, "It is said: where there is a will, there is a way; I add, where there is an aim, there is a will." Do you have the kind of will Frankl is referring to? Do you also have an aim? Where does it appear to be taking you, not just on the horizontal axis but along the vertical axis as well? What does work mean to you, and what *kind* of work (and, by implication, what kind of life) really matters to you?

Now imagine a job or type of work you really want to do. Ask yourself: Would this kind of work help me realize my will to meaning? If so, what do I have to do to get the job? What am I doing now that will help me along the way? What am I doing now that is *in* my way? What could I do now to help me along the way?

No matter what our specific job might be, it is the *work* we do that represents who we are. When we meet our work with enthusiasm, appreciation, generosity, and integrity, we meet it with meaning. And no matter how mundane a job might seem at the time, we can transform it with meaning. Meaning is life's legacy, and it is as available to us at work as it is in our deepest spiritual quests. We breathe, therefore we are *spiritual*. Life is, therefore it is *meaningful*. We do, therefore we work.

As quoted in Plato's *Apology*, the classical Greek philosopher Socrates said, "The unexamined life is not worth living." Doing the kind of meaning analysis I am suggesting is an important part of examining our life. The goal is to follow the ancient Greek aphorism "know thyself," from an inscription at the Oracle of Apollo at Delphi. Surely this knowing takes effort, but the return on investment, as you've seen many times in this book, can be — and usually is — substantial. Meaning analysis offers guidance along the path to self-discovery and personal growth, to help you live and work with meaning, find opportunities to live a truly authentic life, and achieve your highest potential.

Bouvie & Me

Sometimes we find ourselves guided along this path, our labyrinth of meaning, in ways and by guides that may seem a bit unusual but are significant nonetheless. Meaning analysis, in other words, doesn't always have to follow strict rules of logic or comply with the Socratic method. Indeed, our inclinations to discover and clarify meaning, gain insight, and explore alternative ways of being and doing may lead us in unexpected directions. Let me share an example that has had a profound and meaningful influence in my own life.

Over the holidays last year I saw the movie *Marley & Me*, based on the *New York Times* best-selling autobiographical book *Marley & Me: Life and Love with the World's Worst Dog*, by journalist John Grogan. In brief, this is the

sentimental story of a newlywed couple who learn important life lessons from their adorable but naughty, neurotic,
and very much out-of-control dog Marley, a yellow Labrador
retriever. Described as the "world's worst dog," Marley nonetheless grows, both literally and figuratively, into one of the
most important *people* in the Grogan family.

I enjoyed the movie a great deal. Full disclosure: I'm a
dog lover and owner, which makes such a movie more appealing and entertaining, especially for adults. Heck, I still get
tears in my eyes when I think about the ending of the movie
Old Yeller, one of the most memorable films of my early childhood. There must be something special about those old yeller
dogs!

As I said, I have a dog and, like Marley, he's also special
and one of the most important members of *my* family. He
is not yellow, nor is he naughty, neurotic (at least not too
much!), or out of control. I'm talking about Bouvie, a black
and dark gray, Dutch-bred Bouvier des Flandres, who was
born to "royalty" in Europe with the official name of Tynan
Inca van de Duca Vallei. Since many people are unfamiliar
with the Bouvier breed, the household name Bouvie stuck
with him as a way to remember the breed even before Bouvie
arrived in North America at only nine weeks old (and could
be held in one of my hands!).

Also like Marley, Bouvie has without question taught
me many important, meaningful life lessons over the years.
Among other things, unlike the incorrigible Marley, he is
trained as a therapy dog and has proven his weight in gold
(he's now a hundred-pound "lap dog") working closely with
Alzheimer's patients—that is, he provides affection and com-

fort to them. This gives you a good idea of Bouvie's temperament, because a good therapy dog must be friendly, patient, confident, at ease in all situations, and gentle. Moreover, they must enjoy human contact and be content to be petted and handled, sometimes clumsily and aggressively.

However, Bouvie's influence on me and others goes well beyond his official role as a working therapy dog. Like the key messages conveyed in both the book and movie *Marley & Me*, life with Bouvie has been—and continues to be—filled with many meaning moments. Indeed, while he may be only a dog to some people, Bouvie is much more than man's best friend to me. Over and over, he has shown himself to be an exceptionally wise mentor and confidant, during good times and not-so-good times. Just as important, he demonstrates to me that too often I, like many others, become so focused on the many tasks that need to be accomplished day to day that I lose touch with the so-called simple things in life. Indeed, it is always great to have *someone* in your life, like Bouvie, who can help you slow down to regain awareness of what really matters in life, as well as to enjoy life's blessings and meaningful moments. The kind of relationship between Bouvie and me is itself an important source of meaning!

I've learned a great deal from Bouvie. Among other things, I know that he helps to keep me grounded when the complexity of life begins to overwhelm me. As my mentor, he reminds me to appreciate what I have and not fret so much over what I don't have. And as my personal trainer and therapy dog, Bouvie stands ready to coach and guide me to live a simple, healthy, and meaningful life. Of course, it's up to me to listen to his cues.

Here are some of the life lessons—another form of meaning analysis—I've learned from Bouvie so far. To show my respect for Bouvie's innate wisdom, I call these key life lessons the Tao of Bouvie:

The Tao of Bouvie

- Start each day with a happy attitude.
- Greet each person you meet with enthusiasm.
- Delight in the simple joy of a long walk.
- Don't be afraid to stick your head out the window.
- Don't hold grudges for very long.
- Support those in need of a friend.
- Explore everything as you walk through the day.
- When someone is having a bad day, be supportive.
- Take plenty of rests to reenergize so that you are ready for the next adventure.
- Loyalty is a virtue, so be loyal.
- Play is good.
- Food is better (appreciate every meal like it is your last).
- A ball is all you need to feel fulfilled.
- Relieve yourself regularly to help reduce stress.
- Set your limits by marking your spot.
- Accept treats and a kind pat on the head whenever they are offered.
- Protect those you love and who love you.
- Show your passion and enthusiasm with gusto.

- When you see loved ones, act as if you haven't seen them for years.
- Be your authentic self.
- Display love unconditionally.

The real challenge for me, and I suspect for most people, is to act upon and manifest these meaningful guidelines in my own life with consistency and integrity—that is, to *walk* them, not just *talk* about them. I am reminded of a bumper sticker I came across years ago that read, "Be the kind of person that your dog thinks you are!" How appropriate, don't you think? Now what about *you*? What are you learning from your dog or other pet that may be a significant part of *your* life? After conducting your own meaning analysis, what things would you add to the above list?

Viktor Frankl's legacy was one of hope and possibility. He saw the human condition at its worst, with human beings behaving in unimaginably intolerable ways. He also saw human beings rising to heights of compassion and caring in what can only be described as miraculous acts of unselfishness and transcendence. Something in us can rise above and beyond everything we think possible. Our instinct for meaning, in our everyday lives and in our work, is ours right now, at this very moment—as long as we are not prisoners of our thoughts.

> *We must never be content with what has already been achieved. Life never ceases to put new questions to us, never permits us to come to rest. . . . The man who stands still is passed by; the man who is smugly contented loses himself. Neither in creating or experiencing may we rest content with achievement; every day, every hour makes new deeds necessary and new experiences possible.*[97]

Meaning Moment Recall a situation in your personal or work life in which you felt trapped or confined in some way and didn't feel fulfilled (this may even be your situation today). Perhaps you were in a bad relationship. Or perhaps you were working in a job or position that you didn't like. Maybe you were doing work that didn't seem meaningful to you. What, if anything, did you do about this situation? Did you resolve it or did it resolve itself? As you think about the situation now, what did you learn from it? In hindsight, what could you have done differently in this situation?

Meaning Question: In what ways do you find meaning and fulfillment in your personal life and work?

FOR FURTHER REFLECTION

Think about the ways in which you can help your family members, friends, and co-workers unlock personal meaning and fulfillment in their life and work. How would you ask them to demonstrate that they understand their responsibility to stand up to life and work in order to find personal meaning and fulfillment?

The Meaning Difference®

The search for meaning is a megatrend of the twenty-first century. I've made this claim on numerous occasions and have seen it confirmed by many reliable sources with increasing frequency since this book was first released.[98] Indeed, in our so-called postmodern world, there is increasing evidence that people in all walks and stages of life either are on a conscious search for meaning in their everyday lives, including their work lives, or at least they are aware that such a search for meaning is both necessary and desirable for their optimal health and well-being.

Meaning is the energy or fuel that motivates us to achieve our full potential as human beings, in our personal and our working lives. As I pointed out in chapter 11, Dr. Frankl ardently believed that "man's search for meaning is the *primary* motivation in his life and not a 'secondary rationalization' of instinctual drives." As a motivational force, the will to meaning is not external but is intrinsic to our very being—a part of our "soul's code," if you will—which distinguishes it from other human drives, such as those based primarily on pleasure or power (see chapter 5).

Over the years, I've observed how these human motivations play out in many different ways and places. I've also noticed marked differences in the quality of people's personal and working lives that appeared to be associated with, if not the direct result of, these motivations. Other things being equal, people whom I would describe as living or working with meaning as their primary source of motivation appeared to be more passionate, more engaged, and more resilient than those for whom meaning was either off their personal radar screen or was not a targeted destination on their life path.

Again, it is more important to be aware than it is to be smart. An initial step toward a meaningful life, which includes meaningful work (again, I'm defining the notion of work very broadly), is becoming conscious of the basic human need to search for and discover meaning in life and work. And this is a step that each of us must take on our own; nobody else can do it for us.

Let me repeat what may be one of Viktor Frankl's most profound assertions: "I am convinced that in the final analysis, there is no situation that does not contain within it the seed of a meaning." In other words, meaning can be found everywhere, in and through all of life's experiences—more like energy than matter. In this sense, it cannot be created or destroyed, only transformed. It exists in the moment—in *all* moments, as Frankl suggested—and is waiting to be discovered.

Meaning and Purpose

Unlike purpose, meaning is not a destination per se because it doesn't stop when we find it (or at least when we think that we've found it). I do not want to imply that purpose is not important, nor do I want to marginalize its inherent value. Having a purpose—especially one that helps define and guide our life—is of course an important matter. Seeking to clarify and understand our aims in life, in our personal and working lives, are also key elements of the existential (that is, meaning) analysis advanced in this book. Our purpose(s) along life's path, as well as our higher life purpose, are integral parts of the meaning equation. They matter and have a purpose; therefore they have meaning.

However, not everyone may be fortunate enough to find or fulfill their purpose in life. Perhaps their life is cut short by a tragic accident, as a consequence of war or natural disaster, or from an incurable disease. Such misfortunes may leave us wondering about and saddened by lives that did not have the opportunity to realize their full potential. But even though their life *purpose* may not have been fully revealed or fulfilled, it does not mean that their lives did not have *meaning*. On the contrary—and I hope that this central point is clear after reading this book—*all life has meaning*.

Sometimes the meaning in our lives looms big, stares us directly in the eyes (or perhaps in our mind's eye), and therefore is easy to recognize. On other occasions, meaning is less obvious and may even seem insignificant—at least at the time. I call these meaning moments mini-meanings, like the character Mini-Me in the *Austin Power* movies. As Mini-Me was a clone of Dr. Evil in these films, your mini-meanings are still a reflection of you, so try to remain aware of them and discover what they may be telling you. By following the principle of detecting the meaning of life's moments, a string of mini-meanings actually may suggest (or help to identify) a pattern that could result in a larger meaning as well as guide you toward a purpose that may not have been detectable before. I've learned in my own life, sometimes the hard way and with great reluctance, that mini-meanings frequently provide important cues and sources of insight. If we allow ourselves to learn from them, they can stimulate personal growth and development in meaningful ways.

Meaning and Energy

Let me return to the notion of meaning as energy for a moment. As you know, Viktor Frankl named his unique approach to psychotherapy Logotherapy. And he did this for good reason. It is a humanistic form of psychotherapy that paved the way for us to know meaning as a foundation of our existence. In addition, the name Logotherapy distinguishes his school of thought in another, less obvious respect. If you haven't recognized it already, please note the root word *logo* in this name. Frankl chose to name his system of psychotherapy with direct reference to the Greek word *logos* (λογος) for a couple of reasons. One was the fact that the most frequent (though rough) English translation of *logos* as "the meaning" best fit his paradigm of therapy through meaning.

Upon closer examination, the various translations of the word *logos*, a common Greek word, reveal also that it has deep spiritual roots. In fact, the concept of *logos* can be found in most of the great works describing the history of Christianity and throughout the literatures of religion and Western philosophy. One of the first references to *logos* as "spirit" came from the ancient Greek philosopher Heraclitus around 500 BC. The *logos* of Heraclitus has been interpreted in various ways: as "the logical," as "meaning," and as "reason." To Heraclitus, the *logos* was responsible for the harmonic order of the universe, a cosmic law that declared "One is All and Everything is One."

The doctrine of the *logos* was also the linchpin of the religious thinking by the Jewish philosopher Philo of Alexandria, who clearly established it as belonging to the spiritual realm. Indeed, for Philo, the *logos* was divine—it was the source of energy from which the human soul became manifest. Moreover, to Philo, the origins of *logos* as "spirit" and "life energy" were clearly established and well documented in the writings of the early Greek philosophers and the theologians of his era.[99]

It is also no coincidence that the concept (and process) of dialogue, a core methodological component of Frankl's Logotherapy, likewise is grounded in the *logos*. The word *dialogue* comes from two Greek words: *dia* (διά), meaning "through," and *logos*, which we now know can be translated as "meaning" or "spirit."

The process of dialogue takes on a new and deeper meaning when it is perceived as accessing a pool of common spirit (*logos*) through a genuine connection between people. This suggests more than collective thinking or simply arriving at a common understanding or shared meaning of something, although dialogue certainly is a component of such a holistic process. Authentic dialogue enables individuals to acknowledge honestly that each is part of a greater whole, that they naturally resonate with others within this whole, and that the whole is indeed greater than the sum of its various parts.

Furthermore, the energy that accompanies true dialogue cannot easily be denied. We've all been in meetings with co-workers where the conversation was open and authentic, and where mutual respect—even of each other's differences of opinion—and civility were obvious and accepted rules of engagement. The process seemed to unfold naturally without any coercion or management. Everyone was in the flow and it felt good. Then an outsider, perhaps a supervisor or someone not trusted by some or all members of the group, entered the room. What usually happened? How did it feel? I bet that you felt the energy in the room take a deep dive! And the free-flowing communication that everyone had enjoyed shut down, while at the same time personal guards went up and the masks of inauthenticity were put back on. This kind of scenario in the workplace is not that uncommon, is it?

A similar experience happens in our personal lives when transparency and authenticity are replaced by phoniness, secrecy, dishonesty, or hypocrisy. Let's face it: in real life, relationships among family members and friends do not always mirror those ideal role models seen on television, except perhaps for some of the so-called reality shows that seem to base their ratings on featuring dysfunction at its best! And while there is obvious truth in the saying "You can choose your friends but not your family members," we recognize that friendships, even those that purport to be founded on openness and trust, may not always allow the energy associated with honest communication and authentic dialogue to flow freely either.

Against this background, let me suggest that the more people are intrinsically motivated by the search for meaning (as opposed to the external influences of pleasure or power), and therefore are authentically committed to meaningful values and goals (the will to meaning), the more likely it will be that the intentions and process of authentic dialogue will unfold in an ideal way. By the way, this suggestion also applies to the inner dialogue we conduct with ourselves. Put differently, we cannot truly know ourselves, to paraphrase the inscription at Delphi referred to in chapter 11, if we do not have an open and honest authentic dialogue within ourselves.

By injecting the search for meaning into what we say and do, we raise the bar regarding how we relate to ourselves and others. This in turn changes the way that we look at ourselves and the world around us. We bring a new consciousness to our life and work. We bring new energy—a life energy similar to that described for the *logos*—to our life experiences, including the challenges and opportunities, that helps to sustain us as we travel down life's highway, much like the fuel put into the tanks of automobiles and other vehicles that transport us in our routine lives.

For this reason we need to keep track of our meaning "fuel gauge" (see figure 3) to ensure that it does not fall to empty, allowing our lives to stall out, go off the road, or worse. As with our automobiles, we cannot run on empty. For long stretches between rest stops and for unknown or treacherous roads, it is always best to keep the tank as full as possible. When we begin to believe that our lives or our work have little or no meaning, we risk the danger of running on empty. And while we may not be able to readily explain what meaning *means* for us—in our personal or our working lives—we usually know what meaninglessness feels like. We might say we are feeling apathetic, bored, cynical, disenchanted, empty, imprisoned, indifferent, jaded, stuck, unhappy, uninspired, worthless—or add your own descriptors for being in an existential void. We can feel the fuel being sucked right out of us as if someone were draining the gas tank of our car!

Figure 3. The Meaning Difference.

I suspect that for most people, these symptoms of meaninglessness—and the existential angst that usually accompanies them—are not what they desire. Even if they haven't
attained (or ever will attain) self-actualization, as espoused
by the humanistic psychologist Abraham Maslow, this does
not mean that their lives are devoid of meaning. Indeed, we
know now that even Maslow tempered his views on human
motivation near the end of his life. As Dr. Covey revealed
in his foreword to this book, Maslow believed that his needs
hierarchy theory was too needs-determined, and that self-actualization was not the highest need after all. His conclusion
that self-transcendence was the human soul's highest need
reflects more of the spirit of Viktor Frankl, rejecting a reductionist view of human nature and reflecting the concept of
the *logos* introduced in this chapter.

In the final analysis, what I call The Meaning Difference®
accounts for the most significant portion of the variation in
how well people make a life and a living that matters to them.
This variable, which I have tried to capture through the fuel
gauge metaphor, helps to differentiate people, their lives, and

their livelihoods by their capability of dealing with the complexity, challenges, and changes of everyday life and work. Moreover, I have found through my research and practice over many years and through my personal experience that The Meaning Difference® very much influences and helps to explain the degree to which people of all ages and walks of life find fulfillment in their life and achieve their highest potential. Let's now look at some areas of life and domains of work in which meaning makes a positive difference.

Meaning at the Core

As the beginning of this chapter, I asserted that the search for meaning is a megatrend of the new millennium. Whether or not you agree with this bold declaration, one thing is becoming pretty clear: more and more people, especially in the United States and other advanced, affluent countries, are experiencing a shift in consciousness and asking meaning-related questions about their lives. Maybe this focus on meaning is because the world appears to be exceptionally and increasingly unstable. Perhaps it is because many people have a quality of life that is more centered on quantity than quality. Or maybe it is the product of living in a postmodern hall of mirrors in which, no matter how much we have and do to make ourselves happy and fulfilled, we are left in an existential void with no visible means of escape. Who knows?

This book offers an alternative path—one that doesn't replace your current lifestyle but instead seeks to complement it. This path is focused on the search for and will to meaning. Imagine for a moment that you have a compass designed with the dimensions depicted in figure 2 in chapter 11, complete with directional arrows pointing to Meaning, Despair, Success, and Failure. Can you see how you might use such a compass to guide you on your life journey? Can you see how the compass might help you stay on a meaning course and not become sidetracked in your personal life or working life?

Immediately after the first edition of this book was released, I started to receive a flood of communications from readers asking a wide range of existential questions and sharing an equally wide variety of personal and work-related experiences. I was struck immediately by the number of people who were experiencing some kind of existential angst in their life or work. It assured me that my meaning message was resonating with people, often in profound life-changing and life-affirming ways.

Because I am also an academic by training who used to teach classes on applied research methods and statistical analysis, I wanted to add a little rigor to the kind of data I was receiving from people in the field. So from 2005 through 2007 I collected quantitative and qualitative information about the search for meaning in life and work on a more systematic basis. These research efforts were conducted in addition to, and as a supplement to, the mostly narrative information that came to me unsolicited by my readers, clients, and public speaking audiences.

In the spirit of full disclosure, I must admit that these research activities were not as rigorous as I would have liked, for they did not involve any kind of randomized or purposive design (I used to teach this subject at both the undergraduate and graduate levels!). Therefore, the representative nature of my samples is suspect, and I don't want to violate standard research protocol by making any (or at least not too many) inferential leaps from these data. However, if I stick to my findings and offer them as food for thought, the value of what I discovered is noteworthy, practically useful, and hence meaningful. And when I juxtapose such empirical evidence with that found in other studies, this value is measurably enhanced.

Our first effort to gather data was called the Meaning in Work and Life Survey. It was a simple survey, consisting of only seven closed-ended items followed by an open-ended comment section, conducted via e-mail. The respondents simply downloaded the survey from our Web site, responded to the items using a response key, and returned their completed questionnaire by e-mail. During the period we were accepting responses, a total of 242 self-selected individuals responded to the survey. Because the respondents, by their voluntary participation, displayed an interest in the search for meaning in life and work, it is possible that the results were skewed in a way that was more favorable to the meaning issues being addressed than might have been found in a random sample.

Instead of going through the survey results item by item, let me share with you an overview of the key findings. Overall, respondents were much more likely to view their personal life as having meaning than they did their work life. They reported most frequently that they were "excited" about their personal life, and that they contributed to the world in meaningful ways because of and through their personal life experiences rather than their work experiences. For example, one participant said, "My answers to the questions about 'work' pertain to my gainful employment. I do feel passionate about my personal pursuits, which are really what sustain me." Here is another, similar assessment: "While work doesn't always turn my crank, the other parts of my life do. They are what gives it meaning more so than work."

In addition to being less likely to report that their work had meaning, the respondents also suggested through the survey and their comments that creating meaningful work and workplaces was the responsibility of their employer more than of themselves. One respondent observed: "I believe that the work I do is important, and I am committed to it, but I do not believe that my organization values my work, or the way in which I do it." Another respondent shared the following perspective: "There is a need to distinguish between 'work' and 'job.' My 'work' is meaningful to me and, I feel, potentially to others too, but the 'job' in which I currently exercise it is another matter! Insofar as my 'job' defines how other people view me, or how I view myself, it doesn't contribute much 'meaning' to my life (or give me an opportunity for meaningful work)."

These findings suggest that there are plenty of opportunities to help individuals and organizations discover meaning in their work and create environments that support and sustain meaningful work. There are also opportunities to share and leverage the best practices and lessons learned that are associated with the discovery of meaning outside of work. Unless attention is paid to such meaning-related linkages and issues, there is a serious risk of decreased worker engagement, threatening productivity goals, improvement of performance, and innovation, key factors behind any organization's or industry's competitive advantage in the national and global marketplace.

Meaningful Engagement

It is important to view engagement from a meaning-centered perspective because engagement directly influences both our personal lives and our working lives. Moreover, meaning has been found to drive engagement in a wide range of personal and work-related environments. In turn, the power of meaningful engagement drives and sustains satisfaction, performance, creativity, and innovation at the individual and collective levels.[100] Across industries and sectors, there is growing interest among organizations to provide meaningful work, create meaningful workplaces, and deliver meaningful results in terms of experiences, products, and services to a broadly defined community of stakeholders. Finding ways to meaningfully engage employees and allied workers is a strategic necessity to drive business results, build customer loyalty, and make a positive difference in a world in which trust and public confidence in corporations and governments leave much to be desired.

It is not surprising then to learn that in 2009 my meaning-centered work drew the attention of the Gallup Organization, which for a number of years has been studying the employee engagement issue with emphasis on its relationship to productivity. Based on its research, the Gallup Organization identified three types of employees:

1. *Engaged employees* work with passion and feel a profound connection to their company. They drive innovation and move the company forward.

2. *Disengaged employees* are essentially checked out. They're sleepwalking through their work day, putting time—but not energy or passion—into their work.

3. *Actively disengaged employees* aren't just unhappy at work; they're busy acting out their unhappiness. Every day, these workers undermine what their engaged co-workers accomplish. A 2006 Gallup survey found that of all U.S. workers aged eighteen and older, about 20.6 million—15 percent of the total workforce—were actively disengaged! Moreover, Gallup estimated that the lower productivity of actively disengaged workers cost the U.S. economy about $328 billion.[101]

Remember, these findings are for 2006. Imagine what the situation looks like today. How many actively disengaged workers do you think are in the workforce during an economic crisis of global proportions and a time of increasing cynicism among a distrusting public? Here's a hint: the Conference Board released study results in January 2010 revealing that job satisfaction in the United States is at its lowest level in some two decades! According to one of the study's authors, "While one in ten Americans is now unemployed, their working compatriots of all ages and income continue to grow increasingly unhappy." Furthermore, "the downward trend in job satisfaction could spell trouble for the overall *engagement* of U.S. employees and ultimately employee *productivity*" (emphasis added). Another study coauthor, John Gibbons, who is program director of employee engagement research and services at the Conference Board, added the following: "Challenging and *meaningful* work is vitally important to *engaging* American workers"[102] (emphasis added). It looks like the writing is on the wall, and the need for meaningful engagement has never been so urgent and important.

The issue of meaningful engagement is not simply a matter of concern for corporations and other business enterprises in the private sector. On the contrary, this issue reaches across all sectors and industries. Leaders in health-care organizations, for example, are increasingly interested in ways to meaningfully engage employees because both disengaged and actively disengaged workers in health-care settings have an especially negative impact on the quality and costs of service, two issues that are always central to health-care reform.[103]

In addition to health care, another massive human service system isn't working as well as it should and needs attention and improvement. I'm talking about education reform. One would think that a focus on improving the quality of education, along with an investment in educating the public about the fundamental importance of education in creating and sustaining a democratic society, would be no-brainers. Unfortunately, this is not yet the case.

I've had the good fortune of sharing my meaning-centered message with public school systems and other educational entities and of speaking at conferences where the pursuit of excellence in education was the primary theme. In the context of this discussion about engagement, let me share an example. Not long ago, I was the convocation keynote speaker and conducted in-service training for teachers and administrators representing an independent school district in Texas. The topic was Meaningful Improvement: Engaging Minds, Achieving Results. In other words, to be effective and sustainable, education reform needs to be both meaningful and engaging. And once again, the power of full engagement in all of life's pursuits stems from the search for meaning. This basic tenet applies to everyone involved in the educational process—students, parents, teachers, administrators, and the community. In other words, no *person* can be left behind if we expect to see meaningful improvement in our broadly defined education system become a reality.

Coping Skills

Life in the twenty-first century is much more complex than I visualized when I was growing up. By the time we reached that magical year 2000, I imagined that we would all live in a utopian, futuristic world much like that of *The Jetsons*, the popular animated television show of the 1960s. (By the way, a live-action adaptation of Hanna-Barbera's show is currently in preproduction, set for release in 2012 by Warner Brothers!)

So the future is here, and what I had imagined as a child did not come to pass. And yes, we live in uncertain, volatile, fragile, and undoubtedly stressful times. However, why do some people seem more capable of coping with stress and life challenges—even crises outside their control—than others? Moreover, why do some people choose to see the glass of life as half empty while others see it as half full? One person even told me that his glass was not only half empty but it was also leaking!

As I write this, the economy of the United States, along with that of many other countries around the world, is in crisis. Crises, especially those that are beyond our control, not only test our will and coping skills but also provide us with an opportunity to do some soul-searching to reflect seriously on the meaning of our lives, including our work lives. That is, if we find and take the time to do so. By investing time in self-examination and self-discovery, we often can find a silver lining in the crisis we face. For example, let's consider the economic crisis.

According to the *Parade* magazine Crisis Impact Poll conducted in July 2009, "creating a meaningful life" became important to 68 percent of respondents. This did not mean that the other 32 percent were not interested in creating a meaningful life; rather, over two-thirds of the respondents were now conscious of the need to make creating a meaningful life a priority. In addition, 83 percent of respondents reported that they were reconsidering what they actually need in life. These findings were described as the "upside of coping" with the economic crisis.[104] In other words, a positive consequence of the economic crisis was bringing the search for meaning into focus for many people, encouraging them to take meaningful action to cope with the crisis.

Similarly, in an article titled "Giving Meaning to Our Troubled Times," published in the *Greenville (SC) News*, one of the newspaper's columnists decided to apply the Ten Positive Things Exercise in this book and came up with the following list of ways we can gain from the economic crisis. We can:

1. Become more aware of needs versus wants and thus be less wasteful in our spending.
2. Become more sensitive toward the environment, using less energy and fewer natural resources and recycling more.

3. Become more aware of the needs of those most negatively affected by current conditions: the poor, the undereducated, and the unemployed.

4. Become less willing to incur new debt and discover that living within our means brings renewed peace of mind.

5. Recall the satisfaction to be had from living more simply.

6. Save more and consume less. As a result, there will be more capital available to invest in American businesses.

7. Ultimately have a leaner, more productive corporate America which is focused on new and healthier demands of consumers.

8. Become more sensitive to the human condition and to our individual dependence upon one another. And I believe that with a better understanding of the responsibilities of leadership, the United States will become a better example to, and partner with, the rest of the world.

9. For a while at least, become wiser, and more aware of the human attraction to bubbles, the resulting panics, and the destructive emotions of greed and fear.

10. Benefit in countless other ways, as we Americans seem to have a resiliency for rebounding from adversity while becoming stronger, wiser, and better for it.

The author ends the article with the following advice: "A time like this provides a valuable opportunity for a reappraisal of our values."[105]

Resilience

Coping skills, when viewed in their larger context, are part of our resilience, also known as positive adaptation to adversity. While everyone goes through tough times, as mentioned earlier, some people have an easier time coping, navigating them more efficiently and effectively. The secrets of resilient people have become a hot research topic in the wake of such disasters as 9/11, the Asian tsunami, Hurricanes Katrina and Rita, and the Haiti and Chile earthquakes.

Concern about resilience among American soldiers—both those on active duty and those who are transitioning to civilian life—has also become a high priority. For example, in 2009 the U.S. Army established a new resilience program that includes mental fitness training for soldiers to battle growing rates of depression and post-traumatic stress disorder (PTSD). This unique program is part of the army's Comprehensive Soldier Fitness initiative, directed by Brigadier General Rhonda Cornum, PhD, MD.

General Cornum is uniquely suited to direct this program initiative. When she was a U.S. Army flight surgeon, she became one of two American servicewomen taken prisoner in the 1991 Persian Gulf War against Iraq. Her story of resilience helped convince Americans that female soldiers could serve in expanded roles in wartime. She published her memoir about the conflict and her captivity, *She Went to War: The Rhonda Cornum Story*, in 1992. Her inspirational story is much more than an account of personal courage and resilience in the face of significant adversity. Cornum's message is also one of principle-centered honor, enduring love, and deep meaning.

Of course soldiers have to deal with stress in every aspect of their lives. Building on research from the emerging and evolving field of positive psychology, the army is looking for ways to reduce stress among soldiers and their families in order to improve its overall mission through retention, increased resilience, and enhanced soldier performance.

The new resilience program is designed with these strategic aims in mind. General Cornum, it should be noted, brings a new and somewhat controversial perspective on the post-traumatic experience, referred to as post-traumatic *growth*. In a recent interview, she emphasized the positive effects of combat: "Research appears to show that many people can emerge from traumatic experiences with greater confidence, a keener sense of compassion and appreciation for life."[106] Although what determines post-traumatic growth versus PTSD is still largely unknown, there are indications, in line with Frankl's logotherapeutic stance, that the will to meaning plays a significant role in how people emerge from traumatic experiences.

Being a prisoner of war is not the only form of imprisonment that requires resilience to survive and emerge from the traumatic experience in the positive way suggested by General Cornum. Let's consider inmates who are serving time in a state or federal penitentiary for some criminal offense. For months now, I have communicated with a number of inmates in both the United States and Europe who have shared their personal search for meaning during incarceration.

With so much of their personal freedom taken away, these human beings are not only seeking redemption but also are trying to discover the deeper meaning behind their predicament. With time for self-reflection and self-discovery, each of these prisoners sought to describe for me their personal path to meaning. They wrote about their individualized approach to what is effectively a form of meaning analysis, and about their prognosis for living and working with meaning in the future—whether or not they expected to be released from prison.

Each of these prisoners had read the first edition of this book, the title of which is especially apt under such circumstances. One inmate, who is serving a life sentence, said he wants to use his experience to help others. He wrote: "For a long time, I was very bitter and angry about my situation. Then I read your book and really started to look at life with a different perspective. I had been misinterpreting life all along, and am now free of the prison I had created in my own mind." Another inmate, also serving a life sentence, shared the following thoughts: "I have spent my time whilst in custody learning to improve my own life and becoming a better person. I am working hard to address the deeper meaning behind my offending and change my life, as well as gain answers to questions I need from my inner self."

What is common and revealing in these quotations is that even though both prisoners are facing a formidable challenge that no one would like to endure, both demonstrate resilience by being able and willing to explore the meaning of their lives' moments, including those moments that may be extremely painful for them. Moreover, the inmates are demonstrating their willingness to own up to their own lives by discovering the meaning of any given moment, including those that came during their imprisonment.

Health and Wellness

The United States is experiencing massive job losses and the highest unemployment rate in decades. And while workers may feel fortunate — if not authentically happy — to at least be employed, there is increasing evidence that they are not feeling *healthy*.

For example, according to a report by the nonprofit research organization Families and Work Institute (FWI), the percentage of workers who say that they are in excellent health dropped from 34 percent in 2002 to 28 percent in 2008. The FWI's explanation for this drop pointed to "a change among men and higher-income employees due to the uncertainty around the economy and the greater pressure that people are feeling to manage their work and family life." Moreover, one-third of workers reported at least one symptom of clinical depression, and over 40 percent said they feel stressed sometimes, often, or very often. One in five workers revealed that they often or very often have trouble falling asleep; a similar number is taking medication to lower blood pressure; and 14 percent are being treated for high cholesterol. Research has shown that chronic stress at work can worsen unhealthy symptoms such as these, as well as exacerbate existing medical or health-related conditions.

This kind of unhealthy relationship between stress and work doesn't stop at the office. Indeed, the spillover effects can be toxic in one's home and personal life. As a good work–life balance becomes more difficult to achieve, some important components of a healthy lifestyle — such as adequate sleep, healthy meals, and exercise — begin to suffer. More people are unable to take charge of their health at work or outside the workplace, including at home, and general health declines.

It's no wonder that surveys seeking to assess life balance are being conducted across the United States to identify America's "Most Stressed Out Cities." In the most recent national survey (2009), Chicago had the honor of being number 1, meaning that it had the least "life balance" and, by implication, all the associated health-related issues and risks.

In other words, living and working in Chicago is a far cry from living and working on the Greek island of Ikaria, recently named by the National Geographic Society as the latest and perhaps most vital "Blue Zone," or place where the common elements of lifestyle, diet, and outlook have led to an amazing quantity—in terms of longevity—and quality of life.[107] Named for Icarus, who in Greek mythology fell into the sea nearby, this tiny island in the North Aegean Sea has now gained worldwide fame as one of the few places on earth where the population regularly lives past ninety years of age.

In fact, researchers found that Ikaria has the highest percentage of ninety-year-olds (and beyond) anywhere on the planet: one out of three people, both male and female. Also, the residents were found to have about 20 percent lower rates of cancer, 50 percent lower rates of heart disease, 11 percent lower rates of diabetes, and almost no Alzheimer's disease or other dementia. Among the key factors behind these statistics and the unusually long life span of Ikarians are the following: physical activity (exercise) that is a natural part of everyday living and working; a nutritious diet rooted in what is commonly referred to as the Cretan or Mediterranean diet;

an environment that is relatively free of pollutants; and a sense of community that connects people in authentic ways to each other.

In short, the findings from Ikaria clearly demonstrate that our health is directly related to our living habits. The Blue Zone researchers discovered that over the centuries, the natives of Ikaria fostered living habits that reduced stress. We now know through scientific studies that there are many links between stress and illness. Indeed, chronic stress, such as the kind people experience when facing marital, financial, or work-related problems, affects a person's ability to function and may even lower her or his immunity to disease and illness.

The living habits of the Ikarians include a passion for enjoying life to its fullest, and a custom of following their natural biorhythms, such as taking daily naps. From a health and wellness perspective, I don't believe that it is important to know if the Ikarians possess the secret to a longer life or even if vitality is their true aim. Who wants to live longer if you believe that your life sucks or doesn't matter? In the wake of the current economic crisis and other stressors that plague the human condition in the contemporary era, Ikarian living habits offer people around the world—including those living in stress centers such as Chicago—practical guidance for becoming more resilient today, tomorrow, and every day of their lives, whether or not they live past ninety years of age.

In other words, by learning how to navigate better through tough times and by embracing, as the Ikarians do, a lifestyle that supports health and wellness, all people can become more resilient when facing life's challenges. Equipped with the power of resilience, they not only increase the likelihood of mastering any crisis but also expand the opportunity for discovering the deeper meaning of life itself. This opportunity, I would argue, lies at the heart and soul of the Ikarian experience. In the final analysis, age per se matters less than lifestyle; and lifestyle in such an indigenous culture suggests a path to health that is based on an authentic commitment to meaningful values and goals—the will to meaning. Moreover, this meaningful outlook on life is an example of what is being called lifestyle medicine, a meaning-focused approach that holds the promise of transforming the nation's sick-care system into a true health-care system.[108]

Shift in Consciousness

The search for meaning is a megatrend whose time has come. In the world of work, meaning is slowly moving to center stage. The idea of meaning in organizations is gaining acceptance among academics and is finally being viewed as a subject for serious investigation.[109] Business practices are also beginning to recognize and leverage the meaning message, especially with consumers, who now more than ever are shopping not only for value in the traditional sense but also for meaning in a more subjective, intuitive, and emotional way. It's not just a question of spending constraints during an economic downturn; it's also a question of resonating with products and services that matter to them, that touch their soul.

I noticed an illustration of this shift in consciousness during the 2009 holiday season. Hallmark promoted its products with the slogan "Find meaning inside" and television ads that featured a delivery truck prominently labeled MEAN-ING. To me, this was a powerful display of meaningful branding, especially because the company's history and core values are consistent with the message.

There is also evidence that a moral transformation of capitalism may be on the horizon in response to the changes that have been taking place in corporate America. In her book *Megatrends 2010: The Rise of Conscious Capitalism*, Patricia Aburdene, one of the foremost trend trackers in the United States, identifies what essentially is a new awareness about how we live and work in the new millennium. The search for meaning is evident in every chapter of Aburdene's book. She makes a persuasive case that the future of business will rest on its ability (and willingness) to make a profit *and* a positive difference with employees, customers, and the external world. This paradigm—which I call meaningful capitalism—is long overdue. Time will tell if there is sufficient momentum for further transformation. In the meantime, we are all responsible for keeping our eyes on the meaning fuel gauge to ensure that progress continues.

As we have discussed, the personal landscape is also shifting toward more meaning-focused attitudes and behaviors. People in all stages of life are paying increasing attention to the quest for personal meaning.[110] This is an especially healthy development—an upside of crisis—when considered in the context of the dysfunctional symptoms, stress-related illnesses, and existential angst in the world presently.

In summary, discovering meaning in life and work is both a personal and a collective responsibility. We've heard this message ring loud and clear numerous times throughout this book. We've also seen how The Meaning Difference® can play out and make a positive, significant difference in our lives. For this to happen, we must make an authentic commitment not to forget the core message of *why* meaning is so important, *how* meaning can benefit all aspects of our lives, and *what* we must do to discover meaning.[111] Stephen Covey said in his foreword: "To learn something but not to do is really not to learn. To know something but not to do is really not to know." To bring meaning into our lives requires learning, knowing, and then doing. This kind of authentic, action-oriented learning and knowing cannot happen until we are no longer prisoners of our thoughts.

The Meaning Difference

Notes

Chapter 1

1. Viktor E. Frankl, *Man's Search for Meaning: An Introduction to Logotherapy*, 4th ed. (Boston: Beacon, 1992), 113–14.
2. Viktor E. Frankl, *Psychotherapy and Existentialism* (New York: Washington Square, 1967), 122.
3. Viktor E. Frankl, *Viktor Frankl Recollections: An Autobiography* (New York: Plenum, 1997), 53.
4. Personal conversation, Vienna, Austria, August 6, 1996. See also Viktor E. Frankl, keynote address (Evolution of Psychotherapy Conference, Anaheim, California, December 12–16, 1990).
5. See Deepak Chopra, *Unconditional Life: Discovering the Power to Fulfill Your Dreams* (New York: Bantam Books, 1991).
6. Viktor E. Frankl, *The Unheard Cry for Meaning* (New York: Washington Square, 1978), 45.
7. Stephen R. Covey, *The 7 Habits of Highly Effective People* (New York: Simon & Schuster, 1989), 277.
8. Viktor E. Frankl, *The Will to Meaning*, 1985 lecture (available on tape from Zeig, Tucker & Theisen, Phoenix, ISBN: 1-932462-08-2). See also Viktor E. Frankl, *The Will to Meaning: Foundations and Applications of Logotherapy* (New York: Penguin Books, 1988).
9. Viktor E. Frankl, *The Unconscious God* (New York: Washington Square, 1975), 120.
10. Frankl, *Man's Search for Meaning*, 75.
11. Frankl, *Man's Search for Meaning*, 108.
12. Frankl, *Man's Search for Meaning*, 49.
13. Viktor E. Frankl, lecture (Religion in Education Foundation, University of Illinois, February 18, 1963). See also Frankl, *Psychotherapy and Existentialism*, 147.
14. Frankl, *Psychotherapy and Existentialism*, 4.

Chapter 2

15. Frankl, *Autobiography*, 35.

16. Frankl, *Autobiography*, 19. See also Anna S. Redsand, *Viktor Frankl: A Life Worth Living* (New York: Clarion Books, 2006).
17. Frankl, *Autobiography*, 53.
18. Frankl, *Autobiography*, 98.
19. Frankl, *Autobiography*, 53.
20. Frankl, *Man's Search for Meaning*, 147–49.
21. http://www.viktorfrankl.org/e/long_cv.html.
22. See also Frankl, *Man's Search for Meaning*, 117.
23. Frankl, *Man's Search for Meaning*, 75.
24. Stephen R. Covey, A. Roger Merrill, and Rebecca R. Merrill, *First Things First* (New York: Simon & Schuster, 1995), 103.

Chapter 3

25. Frankl, *Man's Search for Meaning*, 115.
26. This ministry of meaning has continued to manifest itself beyond Chappell's efforts to ensure that Tom's of Maine, which became part of the Colgate-Palmolive Company in 2006, maintains its core values, beliefs, and mission as a business enterprise. Tom and Kate Chappell's newest venture, Rambler's Way Farm, continues their passion for creating superior products for a sustainable lifestyle, while at the same time creating a business that can be a positive force for its consumers, workers, communities, and the planet. Rambler's Way Farm is "a company that pays homage to America's rich history as a textile producer, while breathing new life into the domestic wool industry, through our collaboration with farmers and producers around the country." See http://www.ramblersway.com/toms.
27. Roots, the Canadian company cofounded by Michael Budman and Don Green on similar principles, has grown into a multinational fashion empire inspired by the Canadian outdoors. Combining their work with meaning and fun, Michael and Don also made a commitment to make Roots play a leading role in environmental and humanitarian issues. See www.roots.com.

Chapter 4

28. Frankl, *Man's Search for Meaning*, 75.
29. I am indebted to Dr. Myron S. Augsburger for this account. See also Nelson Mandela, *Long Walk to Freedom* (New York: Little, Brown, 1995).
30. Christopher Reeve, *Still Me* (New York: Ballantine Books, 1999), 267.
31. *Larry King Live*, February 22, 1996.

32. Reeve, *Still Me*, 3–4.
33. See Christopher Reeve, *Nothing Is Impossible: Reflections on a New Life* (New York: Random House, 2002). See also Dana Reeve, *Care Packages: Letters to Christopher Reeve from Strangers and Other Friends* (New York: Random House, 1999).
34. Frankl, keynote address (Evolution of Psychotherapy Conference, Anaheim, California, December 12–16, 1990).
35. Frankl, *Psychotherapy and Existentialism*, 3.

Chapter 5

36. Frankl, *Man's Search for Meaning*, 87–88.
37. See, for example, www.thestackeddeck.com; www.wallstreetmost-wanted.com.
38. David Packard, *The HP Way* (New York: HarperCollins, 1995), 82.
39. James Hillman, *The Soul's Code: In Search of Character and Calling* (New York: Random House, 1996).
40. Ann Kerr, "Workers Spurn Retirement," *Toronto Globe and Mail*, February 18, 2002.
41. Rodney Crowell, "Time to Go Inward," *Fate's Right Hand* (Sony Music Entertainment, 2003). I'm indebted to my friend and colleague Stewart Levine for introducing me to Rodney Crowell's music and lyrics. Some people, even though they can clearly see such prison bars, are unwilling to go inward and do something constructive about what they see. Take, for example, the former major league baseball player and manager Pete Rose, whose gambling addiction, a manifestation of the will to pleasure, proved to be his own demise, as he describes in his autobiography, *My Prison Without Bars* (New York: Rodale Books, 2004).
42. Frankl, *Unheard Cry*, 21.
43. Kalle Lasn and Bruce Grierson, "America the Blue," *Utne Reader Online*, October 28, 2000.
44. See Dan Pink, *Free Agent Nation: How America's New Independent Workers Are Transforming the Way We Live* (New York: Warner Books, 2001).
45. TGIF is an acronym for "Thank God It's Friday."
46. Thomas Moore, *The Re-Enchantment of Everyday Life* (New York: HarperCollins, 1996), 126.
47. In Roger Frantz and Alex Pattakos, eds., *Intuition at Work: Pathways to Unlimited Possibilities* (San Francisco: New Leaders Press, 1996), 4.
48. Frankl, *Man's Search for Meaning*, 49.

Notes

217

49. Moore, *Re-Enchantment of Everyday Life*, 11.

Chapter 6

50. Frankl, *Man's Search for Meaning*, 114.
51. Frankl, *Man's Search for Meaning*, 115.
52. See, for example, Phil Jackson and Hugh Delehanty, *Sacred Hoops: Spiritual Lessons of a Hardwood Warrior* (New York: Hyperion, 1995).
53. Frankl, keynote address (Evolution of Psychotherapy Conference, Anaheim, California, December 12–16, 1990).
54. Frankl, *Man's Search for Meaning*, 107.
55. Viktor E. Frankl, *The Doctor and the Soul: From Psychotherapy to Logotherapy* (New York: Random House, 1986), xix.
56. Kathleen D. Ryan and Daniel K. Oestreich, *Driving Fear Out of the Workplace: Creating the High-Trust, High-Performance Organization* (San Francisco: Jossey-Bass, 1998).
57. See, for example, Susan Jeffers, *Feel the Fear and Do It Anyway* (New York: Ballantine Books, 1988); and Alan Downs, *The Fearless Executive* (New York: AMACOM Books, 2000).
58. Frankl, *Man's Search for Meaning*, 135.
59. Mark Gerzon, *Coming Into Our Own: Understanding the Adult Metamorphosis* (New York: Delacorte, 1992).
60. See Frankl, *The Doctor and the Soul*, 26.
61. I'm indebted to Art Jackson for introducing me to this particular exercise.

Chapter 7

62. Frankl, *Man's Search for Meaning*, 125.
63. Frankl, *The Doctor and the Soul*, 118.
64. Frankl, *The Doctor and the Soul*, 118.
65. See Ronna Lichtenberg, *It's Not Business, It's Personal: The 9 Relationship Principles That Power Career* (New York: Hyperion, 2002).
66. Jean Francois Manzoni and Jean-Louis Barsoux, "The Set-Up-To-Fail Syndrome," *Harvard Business Review*, March–April 1998, 101–13.
67. Frankl, *The Doctor and the Soul*, 126.
68. See, for example, Charles C. Manz, *The Power of Failure* (San Francisco: Berrett-Koehler, 2002).
69. Robert Johnson, "Speakers Use Failure to Succeed," *Toronto Globe and Mail*, January 30, 2001.
70. Frankl, *The Doctor and the Soul*, 224.

71. Haddon Klingberg, *When Life Calls Out to Us: The Love and Lifework of Viktor and Elly Frankl* (New York: Doubleday, 2001), 67. See also Frankl, *The Doctor and the Soul*, 232.
72. Frankl, *Man's Search for Meaning*, 128.
73. Frankl, *Man's Search for Meaning*, 127.
74. Frankl, *Autobiography*, 67–68.
75. Frankl, *The Doctor and the Soul*, 224.

Chapter 8
76. Frankl, *Psychotherapy and Existentialism*, 20.
77. The Dalai Lama and Howard C. Cutler, *The Art of Happiness at Work* (New York: Riverhead Books, 2003), 200.
78. *USA Today*, August 19, 2003.
79. Charlotte Foltz Jones, *Mistakes That Worked* (New York: Delacorte, 1991).
80. Rubin Battino, *Meaning: A Play Based on the Life of Viktor E. Frankl* (Williston, VT: Crown House, 2002), 66. See also Frankl, *Man's Search for Meaning*, 54.
81. Frankl, *Autobiography*, p. 98. See also Frankl, keynote address (Evolution of Psychotherapy Conference, Anaheim, California, December 12–16, 1990); Frankl, *Man's Search for Meaning*, 81–82.

Chapter 9
82. Frankl, *The Doctor and the Soul*, 254.
83. Frankl, *The Doctor and the Soul*, 125.
84. See Robert Carlson, *Don't Sweat the Small Stuff at Work* (New York: Hyperion, 1999).
85. See Charles Taylor, *The Ethics of Authenticity* (Cambridge, MA: Harvard University Press, 1991).
86. Frankl, *The Doctor and the Soul*, 255.

Chapter 10
87. Frankl, *Man's Search for Meaning*, 12.
88. Peter M. Senge, *The Fifth Discipline* (New York: Currency/Doubleday, 1994), 13.
89. Haddon Klingberg, "When Life Calls Out to Us: The Love and Lifework of Viktor and Elly Frankl" (speech, Toronto Youth Corps, February 11, 1973), 289.
90. Lovemore Mbigi and Jenny Maree, *Ubuntu: The Spirit of African Transformation Management* (Randburg, South Africa: Knowledge Resources, 1997).

Notes

91. Source unknown; see Elaine Dundon and Alex Pattakos, *Seeds of Innovation Insights Journal*, vol. 1 (2003), 41.
92. Frankl, *Man's Search for Meaning*, 92–93.

Chapter 11
93. Frankl, *Man's Search for Meaning*, 105.
94. Personal conversation, Vienna, Austria, August 6, 1996. See also Frankl, keynote address (Evolution of Psychotherapy Conference, Anaheim, California, December 12–16, 1990).
95. Frankl, *The Will to Meaning* (1985 lecture). See also *The Will to Meaning: Foundations and Applications of Logotherapy*.
96. Frankl, *Psychotherapy and Existentialism*, 27.
97. Frankl, *The Doctor and the Soul*, 130–31.

Chapter 12
98. Alex Pattakos, "Searching for Meaning: Megatrend of the Twenty-first Century," *Personal Excellence*, March 2009, 5; Patricia Aburdene, *Megatrends 2010: The Rise of Conscious Capitalism* (Charlottesville, VA: Hampton Roads, 2005); Gurnek Bains et al., *Meaning Inc.: The Blueprint for Business Success in the 21st Century* (London: Profile Books, 2007). See also Alex Pattakos, "No Person Left Behind: The Search for Meaning in Education," *PA Times* 32, no. 9, Education Supplement (October 2009): 7; Alex Pattakos and Elaine Dundon, "Innovating with Meaning," *Leadership Excellence*, November 2008, 19; and Alex Pattakos, "The Search for Meaning in Government Service," *Public Administration Review* 64, no. 1 (January/February 2004): 106–12.
99. David Winston, *Logos and Mystical Theology in Philo of Alexandria* (Cincinnati: Hebrew Union College Press, 1985). This kind of interpretation of *logos* received attention more recently in Karen Armstrong's best-seller *A History of God*, in which she notes that Saint John had made it clear that Jesus was the *Logos* and, moreover, that the *Logos* was God.
100. Compare Jim Loehr and Tony Schwartz, *The Power of Full Engagement* (New York: Free Press, 2004), which sets out a prescription for managing energy at work based on experience with athletic coaching programs.
101. Gallup Organization, "Engaged Employees Inspire Company Innovation," *Gallup Management Journal*, October 12, 2006.

102. Linda Barrington, Lynn Franco, and John Gibbons, "I Can't Get No...Job Satisfaction, That Is" (New York: The Conference Board, Report Number R-1459-09-RR, January 2010).

103. Eileen E. Morrison, George C. Burke, and Lloyd Greene, "Meaning in Motivation: Does Your Organization Need an Inner Life?" (San Marcos: Texas State University, Faculty Publications, School of Health Administration, 2007).

104. Michael J. Berland and Douglas E. Schoen, "How the Economic Crisis Changed Us," *Parade*, November 1, 2009, 4–5.

105. Gally Gallivan, "Giving Meaning to Our Troubled Times," *Greenville (SC) News*, July 12, 2009.

106. "Combat's Positive Effects Examined," *USA Today*, October 19, 2009. See also Shelly M. MacDonald et al., "Understanding and Promoting Resilience in Military Families" (West Lafayette, IN: Military Family Research Institute, Purdue University, July 2008).

107. Dan Buettner, *The Blue Zones: Lessons for Living Longer from the People Who've Lived the Longest* (Washington, DC: National Geographic, 2008).

108. Mark A. Hyman, Dean Ornish, and Michael Roizen, "Lifestyle Medicine: Treating the Causes of Disease," *Alternative Therapies in Health and Medicine* 15, no. 6 (2009): 12–14.

109. See Joe Raelin, "Finding Meaning in the Organization," *MIT Sloan Management Review* 47, no. 3 (Spring 2006): 64–68.

110. See David Guttmann, *Finding Meaning in Life, at Midlife and Beyond: Wisdom and Spirit from Logotherapy* (Westport, CT: Praeger, 2008). See also Alexander Batthyany and Jay Levinson, eds., *Existential Psychotherapy of Meaning* (Phoenix: Zeig, Tucker & Theisen, 2009); and Michael F. Steger et al., "The Meaning in Life Questionnaire: Assessing the Presence of and Search for Meaning in Life," *Journal of Counseling Psychology* 53, no. 1 (2006): 80–93.

111. Hermann Ebbinghaus, *Memory: A Contribution to Experimental Psychology* (New York: Dover, 1964). This classic work was originally published as *Über das Gedächtnis* (Leipzig: Duncker and Humblot, 1885).

References

Aburdene, Patricia. 2005. *Megatrends 2010: The Rise of Conscious Capitalism*. Charlottesville, VA: Hampton Roads.

Albion, Mark. 2000. *Making a Life: Reclaiming Your Purpose and Passion in Business and in Life*. New York: Warner Books.

Bains, Gurnek, et al. 2007. *Meaning Inc.: The Blueprint for Business Success in the 21st Century*. London: Profile Books.

Batthyany, Alexander, and Jay Levinson. 2009. *Existential Psychotherapy of Meaning*. Phoenix: Zeig, Tucker & Theisen.

Battino, Rubin. 2002. *Meaning: A Play Based on the Life of Viktor Frankl*. Williston, VT: Crown House.

Bulka, Reuven P. 1979. *The Quest for Ultimate Meaning: Principles and Applications of Logotherapy*. New York: Philosophical Library.

Coetzer, Patti Havenga. 2003. *Viktor Frankl's Avenues to Meaning: A Compendium of Concepts, Phrases, and Terms in Logotherapy*. Benmore: Viktor Frankl Foundation of South Africa.

Covey, Stephen R. 1989. *The 7 Habits of Highly Effective People*. New York: Simon & Schuster.

Covey, Stephen R., A. Roger Merrill, and Rebecca R. Merrill. 1994. *First Things First: To Live, to Love, to Learn, to Leave a Legacy*. New York: Simon & Schuster.

Ebbinghaus, Hermann. 1964. *Memory: A Contribution to Experimental Psychology*. New York: Dover.

Fabry, Joseph B. 1968. *The Pursuit of Meaning: Logotherapy Applied to Life*. Boston: Beacon.

Fabry, Joseph B., Reuven P. Bulka, and William S. Sahakian, eds. 1995. *Finding Meaning in Life: Logotherapy*. Northvale, NJ: Jason Aronson.

Frankl, Viktor E. 1967. *Psychotherapy and Existentialism*. New York: Simon & Schuster.

———. 1978. *The Unheard Cry for Meaning*. New York: Washington Square.

———. 1986. *The Doctor and the Soul: From Psychotherapy to Logotherapy*. New York: Vintage Books.

_____. 1988. *The Will to Meaning: Foundations and Applications of Logotherapy*. New York: New American Library.

_____. 1992. *Man's Search for Meaning*. 4th ed. Boston: Beacon.

_____. 1997. *Man's Search for Ultimate Meaning*. New York: Plenum.

_____. 1997. *Viktor Frankl Recollections: An Autobiography*. New York: Plenum.

Gill, Ajaipal Singh. 2000. *Frankl's Logotherapy and the Struggle Within*. Pittsburgh: Dorrance.

Gould, William Blair. 1993. *Frankl: Life With Meaning*. Pacific Grove, CA: Brooks/Cole.

Graber, Ann V. 2003. *Viktor Frankl's Logotherapy: Method of Choice in Ecumenical Pastoral Psychology*. Lima, OH: Wyndham Hall.

Guttmann, David. 2008. *Finding Meaning in Life, at Midlife and Beyond*. Westport, CT: Praeger.

Kimble, Melvin A. 2000. *Viktor Frankl's Contribution to Spirituality and Aging*. New York: Haworth.

Klingberg, Haddon. 2001. *When Life Calls Out to Us: The Love and Lifework of Viktor and Elly Frankl*. New York: Doubleday.

Lasn, Kalle, and Bruce Grierson. 2000. "America the Blue." *Utne Reader Online*, October 28.

Lent, Timothy. 2004. *Viktor E. Frankl Anthology*. Bloomington, IN: Xlibris.

Lukas, Elisabeth. 1984. *Meaningful Living: A Logotherapy Guide to Health*. New York: Grove.

Martin, Mike W. 2000. *Meaningful Work*. New York: Oxford University Press.

McCain, John. 1999. *Faith of My Fathers*. New York: Random House.

Morgan, John H. 1987. *From Freud to Frankl: Our Modern Search for Personal Meaning*. Bristol, IN: Wyndham Hall.

Naylor, Thomas H., William H. Willimon, and Magdaelena R. Naylor. 1994. *The Search for Meaning*. Nashville: Abingdon.

Redsand, Anna S. 2006. *Viktor Frankl: A Life Worth Living*. New York: Clarion Books.

Taylor, Charles. 1991. *The Ethics of Authenticity*. Cambridge, MA: Harvard University Press.

Tengan, Andrew. 1999. *Search for Meaning as the Basic Human Motivation*. Frankfurt, Germany: Peter Lang.

Terez, Tom. 2000. *22 Keys to Creating a Meaningful Workplace*. Holbrook, MA: Adams Media.

Wong, Paul T. P., and Prem S. Fry, eds. 1998. *The Human Quest for Meaning*. Mahwah, NJ: Lawrence Erlbaum.

References

Acknowledgments

If ever a book was more a process than a product, then this must be it. And throughout the process many people contributed, in many meaningful ways, to bringing the final product into being—so many, in fact, that I cannot begin to name them all. Yet some people were especially important in this project—coming to my aid at critical moments in the process—and I would like them to know how thankful I am for their involvement.

Elaine, my wife and business partner, who stood by me through thick and thin, and who helped to keep the flame burning so this book would see the light of day. No words could thank you enough; thanks for being you and for the many, many ways that you contributed to this book.

The Frankl family, who believed in and supported this book project from the beginning. I am forever grateful.

Steve Piersanti, publisher, and Jeevan Sivasubramaniam, managing editor, Berrett-Koehler Publishers, for not giving up on me or this book over so many years, and for ensuring that it was the best product possible.

The entire team at Berrett-Koehler Publishers for believing that the search for meaning in life and work is more than a book.

All my fellow Berrett-Koehler authors, who share a common outlook on creating a world that works for all. Individually and collectively, thanks for making a positive and meaningful difference.

Janet Thomas, who worked hard to turn my ideas into prose and who contributed a writing perspective and expertise that will never be forgotten.

Detta Penna and Sandra Craig, a dynamic designing and editing duo, who made my writing look better than I could have ever imagined.

The various reviewers of my manuscript at different stages, who not only helped to improve the final product but also taught me a lot about myself in the process.

Patti Havenga-Coetzer, friend and colleague, who always keeps Viktor Frankl's spirit alive and well in her heart.

Jeffrey Zeig, for helping to ensure that Viktor Frankl's legacy lives forever.

Clint Walker, also known as "Cheyenne" and the "Big Guy" in *The Dirty Dozen*, who, unbeknownst to him, helped craft my character when my father was on the road. Thank you for reading this book and for continuing to be such an inspiration.

The many readers who shared candid comments about the first edition with me, either directly or indirectly through such channels as online book reviews. The feedback and suggestions proved to be invaluable when I was drafting the revisions now included in the second edition.

Those readers of my articles published in print or posted on blog sites—including featured contributions to the *Huffington Post*, *Fast Company*, Basil & Spice, the Global Dialogue Center, and other popular sites—who shared with me their perspectives on and experiences with the search for meaning in their personal and work lives. What a truly global village and community of practice you proved to be. I'm indebted to each and every one of you for the invaluable, meaningful lessons you taught me.

My clients and students over the years, who by sharing their thoughts and experiences, helped me express and practice the ideas now in this book. Your individual and collective influence on my personal will to meaning cannot be overestimated, nor will it ever be forgotten.

My dog, Bouvie, for being more than man's best friend. Thank you for being my wise mentor, personal trainer, therapist, confidant, and guide on the path to a simple, healthy, and meaningful life. And of course thank you for your unconditional love.

Finally, I want to thank all my other friends, colleagues, and members of my extended family for their encouragement of my work, even if they didn't quite understand at first what I was doing when I told them that I was on a search for meaning. Since the initial release of this book, I'm pleased to report that they now understand what my search is about and, more important, they continue to support my efforts to share this meaning-centered, life-affirming message around the world. Thank you so much for joining me on the human quest for meaning!

Index

About the Author

Carolyn Wright, The Photography Studio, Santa Fe

Alex Pattakos, PhD, affectionately nicknamed "Dr. Meaning," is the founder of the Center for Meaning, based in Santa Fe, New Mexico, USA. He is passionate about helping people realize their highest potential and find authentic meaning in their life and work, as well as helping organizations in all sectors and industries create meaning-centric workplaces and deliver products and services that make a positive difference and are truly meaningful. A former therapist and mental health administrator, he has also been a political campaign organizer, community/economic development policy planner, and full-time professor of public and business administration. He has worked closely with the White House under three presidents on health, education, human services, economic development, and other public policy matters, and has served as an advisor to the commissioner of the U.S. Food and Drug Administration. He was also one of the initial faculty evaluators for the Innovations in American Government Awards Program at the John F. Kennedy School of Government, Harvard University, and has been a faculty member at the Brookings Institution. He is a past president of Renaissance Business Associates (RBA), an international, nonprofit association of people committed to elevating the human spirit in the workplace. During his tenure as president, RBA was active in Australia, Canada, Europe, Nigeria, South Africa, and the United States.

Dr. Pattakos is a passionate speaker (after all, he's Greek!) and is known around the world for his high energy, inspiration, and dynamic approach to engaging participants and effecting change at all levels. As a personal coach and mentor, he works closely with executives, athletes, celebrities, workers from all sectors, retirees, and others to help them find deeper meaning in their everyday life and work and to realize their highest potential. He's also an experienced radio show host, newspaper columnist, and featured contributor to several popular blogs.

For further information:
Center for Meaning
223 North Guadalupe Street, #243
Santa Fe, New Mexico 87501-1868, USA
e-mail: info@prisonersofourthoughts.com
www.prisonersofourthoughts.com

About Berrett-Koehler Publishers

Berrett-Koehler is an independent publisher dedicated to an ambitious mission: Creating a World That Works for All.

We believe that to truly create a better world, action is needed at all levels—individual, organizational, and societal. At the individual level, our publications help people align their lives with their values and with their aspirations for a better world. At the organizational level, our publications promote progressive leadership and management practices, socially responsible approaches to business, and humane and effective organizations. At the societal level, our publications advance social and economic justice, shared prosperity, sustainability, and new solutions to national and global issues.

A major theme of our publications is "Opening Up New Space." They challenge conventional thinking, introduce new ideas, and foster positive change. Their common quest is changing the underlying beliefs, mindsets, and structures that keep generating the same cycles of problems, no matter who our leaders are or what improvement programs we adopt.

We strive to practice what we preach—to operate our publishing company in line with the ideas in our books. At the core of our approach is *stewardship*, which we define as a deep sense of responsibility to administer the company for the benefit of all of our "stakeholder" groups: authors, customers, employees, investors, service providers, and the communities and environment around us.

We are grateful to the thousands of readers, authors, and other friends of the company who consider themselves to be part of the "BK Community." We hope that you, too, will join us in our mission.

A BK Life Book

This book is part of our BK Life series. BK Life books change people's lives. They help individuals improve their lives in ways that are beneficial for the families, organizations, communities, nations, and world in which they live and work. To find out more, visit www.bk-life.com.

Be Connected

Visit Our Website

Go to www.bkconnection.com to read exclusive previews and excerpts of new books, find detailed information on all Berrett-Koehler titles and authors, browse subject-area libraries of books, and get special discounts.

Subscribe to Our Free E-Newsletter

Be the first to hear about new publications, special discount offers, exclusive articles, news about bestsellers, and more! Get on the list for our free e-newsletter by going to www. bkconnection.com.

Get Quantity Discounts

Berrett-Koehler books are available at quantity discounts for orders of ten or more copies. Please call us toll-free at (800) 929-2929 or email us at bkp.orders@aidcvt.com.

Host a Reading Group

For tips on how to form and carry on a book reading group in your workplace or community, see our website at www. bkconnection.com.

Join the BK Community

Thousands of readers of our books have become part of the "BK Community" by participating in events featuring our authors, reviewing draft manuscripts of forthcoming books, spreading the word about their favorite books, and supporting our publishing program in other ways. If you would like to join the BK Community, please contact us at bkcommunity@ bkpub.com.